47
Ways To
Sell Smarter

JIM MEISENHEIMER

A HELBERN BOOK

Helbern
Published by the Helbern Group
Libertyville, Illinois 60048, U.S.A.

Helbern Group, Registered Offices:
Libertyville, Illinois

First Helbern Printing, January 1994
10 9 8 7 6 5 4 3 2 1

Printed in the United States of America

Library of Congress Catalog Card Number: 93-78918

ISBN 0-9637479-0-8

To Bernadette, for your incredible support, encouragement and love. You made this book possible.

Here's what they say:

Continuous learning is the minimum requirement for success in selling today. Jim Meisenheimer has written a fast-moving, results-oriented book full of practical tips and ideas that every salesperson should read, digest and practice - every single day.

Brian Tracy
Author - *Maximum Achievement*

The main reason we salespeople need training is so we can sell smarter. There are lots of books out there that can help us if we had the time to read them all. Jim Meisenheimer saves us time by focusing on what he feels are the 47 best ways to sell smarter.

Homer Smith
Editor, *Master Salesmanship*

The tendency is to gobble up all 47 Ways in one sitting. Don't. Study, savor, and apply them, one at a time to get the greatest impact. Regardless of your skill or experience level, Jim Meisenheimer's droplets of wisdom will help you be your absolute best in sales, and help you increase your income.

Art Sobczak
President, Business By Phone, Inc.

What depth. What breadth. What uniqueness of ideas. Thank you. . .for your comprehensive book. . .guiding all of us who sell for a living . . .in exciting new directions.

Arnold "Nick" Carter
Nightingale-Conant Corporation

Contents

#1

Three Types Of Sales Reps

There are three types of sales representatives. Most of us don't really like labels especially when they may apply to us. But this one really fits. After twenty five plus years in sales it seems that sales reps fall into one of these three categories.

- ⇨ Learning their talk
- ⇨ Talking their talk
- ⇨ Walking their talk

Every person who decides to become a professional sales representative is faced with all the initial challenges of any new job plus some. In almost every sales training class, new sales reps will immediately focus on what they will say to the customers they'll soon be calling on.

For a new sales representative, learning the talk is an exciting time, even though they place too much emphasis on the *talk* and too little on the learning of everything else. It's during this phase that corporate policy and culture should be identified. Customer requirements and industry knowledge are essential learning blocks for all new sales people.

The second category of sales reps are the ones who really like to talk their talk. In fact, they enjoy talking so much, they seldom get the prospect or customer to open up. For some reason, talking is the aspirin for the headaches they get when they start selling. New sales people are often so insecure and nervous, they seem preoccupied with telling their customers how little they know. New sales reps try to impress their customers instead of trying to get to know and understand them.

As a new sales rep, the problem with talking your talk is that most customers realize that you're new and they are generally very patient. So, if you're not on your toes, you'll get positive reinforcement for an undesirable quality. This is confirmed by a 1990 survey of Fortune 500 buyers who said one of their biggest problems with sales reps is that they talk too much. I've never seen a survey that accused sales people of listening too much.

The professional sales representative that walks his talk is the one you should model yourself after. Walking your talk means asking questions before giving answers, it means listening carefully to customer responses and paying special attention to the non-verbal responses. Walking your talk also means taking the time to uncover very specific customer needs and, then and only then, relating the value of your products. It also means when it's time to ask for the decision, you ask. Walking your talk usually means lots of extra work. You can't make selling look easy until you work very hard at it.

Give every man thy ear, but few thy voice.
William Shakespeare

If I had kept my mouth shut, I wouldn't be here.
Sign under a mounted fish

The friends who listen to us are the ones we move toward and we want to sit in their radius.
Karl Menninger

Listen long enough and the person will generally come up with an adequate solution.
Mary Kay Ash

It is better to remain quiet and be thought a fool than to speak and remove all doubt.
Anonymous

#2

Crafty, Cranky, or Crazy?

There are many different ways to characterize customers. Some can be very complimentary and others less so. What's important is not what we call them, but that we recognize that they come in many varieties. One thing is for certain, we'd be lost without them. We'd also be out of gainful employment.

It may come as a surprise to some that customers actually started out as people. Like us, they have dreams, families, problems, job related anxieties, and even the secret desire to change jobs occasionally.

So we have a lot in common with them. Big deal. We probably share more differences than similarities. One mistake we should never make is to put labels on them. We shouldn't be too quick to judge them. Actually, they're very different from each other and we run a big risk if we treat them all alike.

As customers or prospects, they all don't share an equal passion for rock-bottom pricing. They all don't have an interest in making sales people squirm. Most customers don't really subscribe to a win - lose negotiating style. And, despite what many sales reps believe, customers don't

4

always think like each other. Someone once said, "Generalizations obscure differences." When it applies to your customers, truer words were never spoken. Labels belong on soup cans not on your customers.

The next time a customer or prospect starts acting crafty, cranky, or even crazy, see if you're able to identify the real reasons for their behavior. Ask questions. Ask really good questions that will uncover hidden agendas, product concerns, company issues, and perhaps something you inadvertently did to create this unusual behavior.

In relationship selling it's very important that we learn as much as we can about our customers. Backgrounds, interests, education, aspirations, families, goals, and even idiosyncrasies yield knowledge and insight that can often provide the real keys to success.

Remember, when you start to treat all customers alike, your customer's perception of you will take on the characteristics of all the salespeople they deal with. Labels breed labels. By finding out how each customer is unique, you'll establish yourself as a unique sales rep.

Anybody who is any good is different from anybody else.

Felix Frankfurter

People are born equal but they are also born different.

Erich Fromm

Working with people is difficult, but not impossible.

Peter Drucker

The first and greatest commandment is, don't let them scare you.

Elmer Davis

Before you give somebody a piece of your mind, make sure you can get by with what you have left.

Anonymous

Competition doesn't create character, it exposes it.

Anonymous

#3

If Little Things Are So Important,
Who's Counting?

There's an old saying that little things mean a lot. It's been said that in sales this is untrue. In sales, little things are *paramount*. Isn't it the little things that you remember - whether they are positive or negative? Every day we see examples of how important the little things can really be to us. What many sales people fail to remember, in the normal course of doing business, is that their prospects and customers are very perceptive and receptive to the little things that can be done for them.

As a part of your selling efforts, how many specific little things do you routinely do for your customers and prospects? List them on a sheet of paper. How many can you think of quickly? What does it mean if you have to stop and try to recall the little things you're doing for your customers? It could mean that there's an opportunity to do more for your customers.

Let's look at the steps in the selling process and identify just a few little things you can do. When you're prospecting for new business what can you do to differentiate yourself? Can you be creative in the way you seek an appointment? Can you take the time to prepare your telephone call to make it sound professional and to the point? How about that first meeting and your very first impression? You could make an extra effort to create the very best first impression every time you make a cold call.

When you're trying to discover your prospect's or customer's needs, you could prepare a number of questions designed to get them talking. If you must submit a proposal, aren't there some things you could do to create a more positive response, like providing a list of benefits before you show the price?

Another little, yet very important, thing you can do is to prepare in advance how specifically you will ask for the order. One of the most personal and positive things you can do is to send a handwritten note after the sales call even if you don't get the order. Your personal attention can make a big impact. It worked for George Bush, who was a master when it came to sending little notes throughout his career.

Little things mean everything, but only if you take the time to do them.

Application...

Prepare a list of at least ten little things you can incorporate into your sales strategy.

#4

How Do Your Customers Perceive Your Competitors?

When you look into a mirror what do you usually see? Of course, you see the ideal sales representative. A very professional version of the 21st Century variety of the super peddler. You may see yourself as a skilled communicator, a superlative listener, and even as a great problem solver.

You may further imagine a keen ability to discover customers' needs and the ability to establish incredible rapport, time after time. You may even see yourself as the answer to your customers' problems. When it comes to the competition - well there really isn't any top flight competition is there? No, the competition usually just talks about price. Don't you wish they'd stop that nasty habit?

Why is our view of the competition usually limited to our personal opinion which may have little or nothing to do with our customers' real perception of your competition? The reason probably has to do with that three letter word *ego*. Does it ever create a selling blind spot for us? Not only can it create a blind spot, it can spell big time trouble if we underestimate the strengths of the competition and overestimate our own.

The best way to measure your competitor's perception is not to filter it through your ego, but rather to go directly to your customers. Wouldn't you like to know what your customers really liked most and liked least about each of your significant competitors? How could that information impact your account strategies and tactics? How could the knowledge of an individual customer's perceptions shape your own behaviors and sales performance with this customer?

If perception is reality, shouldn't we check on our customers' perceptions? Shouldn't we learn about their hot buttons and about those things they'd like to change with respect to our major competitors? Here are two basic questions to ask:

- ☞ What do you like most about competitor X?
- ☞ If you could change any single thing about competitor X, what would it be?

Don't assume you're already the best. Work diligently at becoming better and better. You can jump-start the selling process if you focus on learning what your customers like and dislike about your competition.

Application...

Identify a list of customers to whom you can ask the above questions.

#5

The Biggest Propeller To Successful Selling

It's not closing. Closing is very important though. It's not handling objections. You should, however, know how to effectively deal with the most common objections. It's not persistence. Most successful sales representatives are very persistent.

The absolute single most important determinant to selling success rests in your ability to establish written goals for your business and life. Before you shrug this off too easily, consider the following. It was recently reported that three percent of the American population have specific goals and have them in writing. Do you think these people represent the most successful or least successful segment of our population?

During the first six years of my sales training business I've worked with over 19,000 salespeople. Whenever I'm talking about the importance of goals, which is almost always, I ask two questions.

☞ How many of you have goals?
☞ If you have goals, are they in writing?

The response to the first question is a universal all hands up.

Everyone has goals or so they imagine. When asked the second question, only about 3% raise their hands. Isn't it amazing?

Stop. Stop. Stop. Stop. Stop. Stop. Stop. Stop thinking that you can have goals, be goal oriented, and be very focused without having very, very, very, very, very, specific goals - committing those specific goals to writing and putting time frames to them. It's not a goal if it isn't in writing. It's nothing more than a dream or a wish. Now, dreaming and wishing are okay as long as we don't confuse them with having goals. A goal must satisfy a minimum of three criteria:

1. It must be very specific.
2. It must be in writing.
3. It must have a deadline.

It is basic and easy to comprehend and not too difficult to actually do, and yet 97% of all Americans don't do it. If you want to achieve something worthwhile and realistic, you must begin by transforming your dreams into goals. You will certainly be an achiever if you follow the three steps above. The final comment is this. I've done it both ways. It changed my life. Enough said.

Application...

Set three specific goals to writing with deadlines ASAP.

No one ever accomplishes anything of consequence without a goal . . . . Goal setting is the strongest human force for self-motivation.

Paul Myer

The will to win is worth nothing unless you have the will to prepare.

Anonymous

A goal is nothing more than a dream with a time limit.

Joe L. Griffith

#6

The Dynamic Impact Of Platoon Selling

One of the largest corporations in America today is IBM, or Big Blue as it's sometimes called. Talk to most IBM customers and they'll tell you how difficult it is to have a business relationship with only one IBM person. It's practically impossible.

Whether you're a prospect or a customer you can expect to see a platoon of IBM types during the course of doing business with them. It may include a team of sales reps, a team of sales managers, a team of installers, a team of technicians, a team of service people, a team of senior managers, or a team comprised of any combination of the teams listed.

As a customer you get a sense that IBM cares. When you think of IBM from a customer's perspective, it's hard to think in terms of one person. You usually think in terms of a platoon of people all trying to help you in as many ways as they can.

If you feel that only big companies with the resources of an IBM can afford to sell in this platoon mode, think again. Even if you work for a smaller firm, with a little effort you can create a very positive platoon sales perception. Here's how to do it.

1. Get management to meet your customers.
2. Let your customers know who handles service.
3. Make sure they know the name of the delivery driver.
4. They should also know customer service personnel by name.
5. Customers should know accounts receivable personnel by name.
6. Tell customers who the key executives are.
7. Introduce them to product managers.
8. Tell them who your quality person is.
9. Introduce them to key administrative people.

The more people your customers know, the bigger you'll appear to be. The more contacts they have, the more comfortable they'll feel. The greater the interaction between your customers and others within your own company, the stronger the partnership. Today IBM is relearning what they invented. Business relationships between companies shouldn't be one dimensional nor limited to the sales rep and the buyer.

You can simulate platoon selling by giving customers organization charts that include names and telephone numbers, providing brochures that include photographs of key staffers, arranging visits, setting up conference calls, and initiating periodic correspondence from different functional areas. When you're trying to close a sale, remember it's more difficult to say no to an entire platoon than it is to one sales rep.

Application...

Plan a way to involve more people with your customers.

> We often have to put up with most from those on whom we most depend.
> **Baltasar Gracian**

> People are lonely because they build walls instead of bridges.
> **Joseph Fort Newton**

> The old saying, "It's not what you know, but who you know," can be changed to, "It's not who you know, but who you know and how well you get along with them."
> **Joe L. Whitley**

#7

Strategic Horoscope

How would you like to determine your selling results by looking for the answers in your daily newspaper's horoscope column. Sound crazy? It may be closer to reality than you think, if you're not strategically planning your sales effort.

There are two principle ways to plan. One is for the short term and the other is for the long term. For sales people, the short term cycle is less than a year, and is often three months. Long-term planning refers to one year or more. This planning if done properly should encompass thinking, writing, and doing (action) if specific results are expected.

Before I share my ideas on planning, it should be noted that too often we are in such a rush to reach our objectives, we fail to set aside quality time to adequately plan how we'll achieve these objectives. This lack of strategic thinking deters from the obvious focus that results from a carefully conceived plan. At least once a year professional sales representatives should dedicate a minimum of one day to strategically think about their business. Don't be too quick to say you're already doing it. Most sales reps acknowledge they think about their territories and customers daily. When pressed, most will admit they don't have time to creatively think about blue sky scenarios that may happen a year from now. If you can't devote one solid day for unrestrained creative thinking, don't think about aiming for the stars. Your best bet is to wait for a shooting star to come your way.

If you commit to one day, I'll help you to invest it wisely. Here are several things to consider. First, to stimulate your creative juices, do your thinking in new surroundings. Go to the library, use someone else's home, stay an extra day if you're out of town. Remember, familiar surroundings won't increase your level of creativity and may even inhibit it, especially if you're faced with interruptions.

The only tools you'll need are a yellow lined legal pad and some pencils. If you have a notebook computer and can spin your "what if" scenarios on it, bring it along. Remember, the purpose is to creatively think about your business. This isn't a "fill in the blanks" exercise.

The process begins and ends with six critical questions. These questions are directed at your business, your territory, your accounts, your customers, and naturally your competitors. These questions will raise more questions and you should consider this process a success if you end up with more questions than answers. While it's tough to digest, questions are more important than answers. Our wisdom grows in proportion to the questions we ask, not the answers we give. Your business landscape will become multi-dimensional when you ask questions. Here are the six questions.

1. Where are you now?
Where are you in your sales expertise and selling skills? Isn't it frightening to think about the implication of working

a full year without learning any new selling skills? How's your performance? What's your relative rank within your region and within your company? What kind of overall growth do you have in your territory and in your top ten accounts? Where are you making inroads in competitive accounts? Where are your competitors making inroads in your accounts? How well are you managing your time and territory? What are your biggest challenges and what are your best opportunities? How specifically have you grown personally and professionally during the last twelve months?

2. Where are you headed if you don't change anything?
What's the implication for you if you don't acquire new selling skills? What happens to your overall performance next year if you don't make up for the loss of your second largest customer? If you don't grow your business at a certain rate, what impact will it have on your overall rank within the sales force? How will your customers react to a strategy that really is based on the "more of the same" concept, especially when your competitors are turning up the burners? With more work and less time available, how will you manage next year when your business is supposed to grow ten percent across the board? What are the risks, if any, if you continue to pass up professional sales development opportunities because of a lack of time? If you could handle all of last year's challenges and opportunities, how well positioned are you to respond to next year's?

3. Where should you be headed?
Do you have specific personal and professional goals? Are these goals very specific and clearly defined? Are they in writing? Do they all have deadlines? For each of your top ten accounts do you have specific objectives for sales,

margins, growth rates, product mix, etc? Have you established specific targets for year-end finish relative to major prospect accounts including sales and time frames? Have you made a commitment to read sales books and to subscribe to sales publications? (See page 141.) Have you planned a way to profile your major customers and prospects? Have you analyzed your travel time and your time devoted to large, medium and small accounts?

4. How will you achieve your objectives?
You really can't "do" a goal or an objective. What you can and must do is to lay out an action plan detailing how specifically you plan to achieve the goals you outlined when considering question three. For example, if your goal is to increase your sales by 12% in your largest account, how will you do it? What are your specific strategies to the **how** question? While your goals define your targets, your strategies drive your actions and ultimately your results. Without proper linkage between goals and strategies, your goals begin to look like dreams.

5. What are the specific details involved?
The details refer to the who, what, where, why, when, which, and how as they relate to initiating and implementing your strategies. Ben Franklin once said, "Small leaks can sink big ships." In sales little things have big impacts.

6. What should you measure?
What gets measured gets done. To keep you on your stated course (objectives) how will you measure your progress? What key elements of success should you review monthly? How and what will you evaluate throughout the sales year to ensure your success?

These questions can make a significant contribution to your selling results, but only if you invest the time to ask them. The favorite day of the week for procrastinators is tomorrow. Action oriented people, the real doers in life, recognize that if you focus your energy on today, tomorrow will take care of itself. The future is yours to live one day at a time. The shape of your future depends on the foundation of your plan.

Are you planning your future or saving the future to plan? It's a clear choice and it's all yours.

> **All worthwhile men have good thoughts, good ideas and good intentions - but precious few of them ever translate those into action.**
>
> **John Hancock Field**

> **Man's actions are the picture book of his creeds.**
>
> **Ralph Waldo Emerson**

It is well with me only when I have a chisel
in my hand.

Michelangelo

All the beautiful sentiments in the world
weigh less than a single lovely action.

James Russell Lowell

Show me a thoroughly satisfied man, and I
will show you a failure.

Thomas A. Edison

#8

Learning Behind The Wheel

When it comes to cars and driving, one thing is certain: the roads aren't getting wider and faster. The cars themselves are getting better - more comfortable, more luxurious, and more electronically equipped. Aren't we fortunate, considering how much time we spend behind the wheel?

We do everything in cars, don't we? The professional sales representative certainly does. Consider the inconspicuous trunk. For a sales rep it becomes a sealed office holding files, samples, company literature, and computer disks, as well as the spare tire.

Many people are eating one or more meals in their cars. Some of us like to relax and listen to our favorite music or radio talk show. We can make telephone calls, send FAXES, and even use our notebook computers in our cars.

How many of us, though, are learning in our cars? What would be the personal and professional impact if we invested only 1% of our lives listening to motivational, inspirational, and educational tapes while driving our cars. Look at it this way. How much of our adult lives should be dedicated to learning?

Since we're spending more time in our cars, shouldn't we attempt to make it more productive? The audio tape has revolutionized the opportunities for self-development. With books on tape, speeches on tape, and focused training programs on tape, now more than ever it's possible to turn auto "dead time" into productive "learning time."

Experts tell us that to get the real benefit from an audio tape it should be replayed to allow key points to be reinforced. This repetition is essential to the learning process.

When you invest fifteen minutes a day in your personal development it represents 1% of your life. Another possible way to view this is to ask, what kind of a person could you become if you committed fifteen minutes each day listening to audio tapes related to the field of professional selling.

To activate your tape library call the Nightingale-Conant Corporation at 800-525-9000. They are the world's largest and most professional supplier of audio tapes.

Take advantage of those increasing driving times. Turn your radios off, turn your tapes on, and if you do this consistently, you'll develop a very significant strategic selling edge.

#9

How To Avoid Sounding Pathetic

Don't say . . .

What are your needs?
I was in the area. . .
We're the best in the business.
Is price important to you?
Are you the decision maker?
What do you think?
When will you make a decision?
Have you looked at the information I sent you?
We are very price competitive.
I see your point, but. . .
What time would be good for you?
When can you let me know?
Can I call you in two weeks?
Are you having any problems with . . .
Can I help you?
I don't know.
We can't do that.
Hang on a minute.
It's our company policy . . .
What do I have to do to earn your business?
Did you get the information I sent?
What do you have for me today?

So, what do you think?
I need you to . . .
You'll have to . . .
I was wondering . . .
I think maybe I can . . .
How soon do you need it?
I'm not sure . . .
Did you get a chance to look at the proposal?
What's going on?

Note: The words you use, build the image you leave behind.

The voice is a second face.
                              Gerard Bauer

Self-expression must pass into communication for its fulfillment.
                              Pearl S. Buck

Every word is like an unnecessary stain on silence and nothingness.
                              Samuel Beckett

#10

Success ... P³ Style

It's been said that selling is easy if you work hard at it. If that's true, why do so few sales representatives make the commitment to work hard and succeed? Perhaps they're missing the magical formula. Remember how early on in our education we were told the virtues of the three R's? Well, it's time to graduate to the three P's. If you follow the three P's, you'll reach the highest selling plateau.

The three P's are preparation, practice, and professionalism. Success in real estate is often attributed to location, location, and location. Success in selling will often follow *focused* preparation, preparation, and preparation. While preparation should be a common sense and routine part of the selling process, often times it's no more than a misplaced priority. Pressure filled days, extensive windshield time, and the desire to get everything done often doesn't allow much time for preparation.

An old military motto says "prior preparation prevents poor performance." Here's what you must prepare to be really effective.

Every sales call should have a prepared objective in writing. To identify a customer's needs, solid open-ended questions should be prepared in advance. When presenting a product's features, be certain that benefits have been prepared in advance. In most selling situations, objections can be anticipated; if they are, your responses to them should be prepared in advance. Asking for the order is never easy; that's why 62% of all sales reps never ask. Maybe more would ask if they prepared in advance how they planned to do it. To be prepared means it's in writing. Anything less just doesn't count.

The second P is practice. Sound strange? It shouldn't. Wherever you see the word professional, you'll see people practicing their craft. Professional athletes, actors, doctors, lawyers, and dentists all must practice their skills to be considered a qualified professional. Sales reps can practice too. They can actually practice on a daily basis if they are committed. There are four key ways to practice. There's self talk, mirror talk, audio talk, and video talk. Speaking out loud to yourself, into a mirror, into a tape recorder, or even into a video recorder will have a dramatic effect on your selling skills and results. Just try it.

The last P is professionalism. If you're prepared and if you've practiced your skills, you're on your way. Being a professional means being an expert. It usually means the top rung on the ladder. It also means you'll be doing a lot of things that the vast majority of all reps are too lazy to do.

The three P's are your connection to success. Just do it!

There are four steps to accomplishment: Plan Purposefully. Prepare Prayerfully. Proceed Positively. Pursue Persistently.

Anonymous

He who every morning plans the transactions of the day, and follows out that plan, carries a thread that will guide him through the labyrinth of the most busy life.

Victor Hugo

For everything you must have a plan.

Napoleon

People who fail to plan, have planned to fail.

George Hewell

#11

What Your Customers
Look For In Your Products

How could you really discover what your customers are looking for in your products? Well, certainly you could ask. That's right, you could ask every single prospect and customer this question. "What specifically are you looking for in our products?" Do you know what all of them will say? Only after you ask the question can you presume the answer.

Why is it so many of our customers never hear the question that allows us the benefit of their answers? Time is a big factor. There isn't enough, so we naturally cut corners. We miss out on an incredible opportunity to talk with customers about the very things that potentially interest them the most about our products. In the process of cutting corners, the buyer and seller usually resign themselves to talking about price.

How many ways would you benefit from knowing what your customers are looking for? How much more personalized would your presentations be, if you took the time to ask your customers about their interests and preferences concerning your products?

Here's a list of things your customers may be interested in.

Specifications	Packaging	Reliability
Quality	Durability	Size
Delivery	Warranty	Color
Operating manual	Service	Price
Accessories	User manuals	Benefits
Installation	Contracts	Service
Appearance	User friendly unit	Features
800 Toll free		

If these are items they're interested in, shouldn't you spend more time talking about these things. As you can see, price is only one parameter in a long list of a customer's interests. How you build value really depends on how well you pinpoint a specific customer's interests. Stop selling your price. Start learning more about what your customer wants.

Application...

Prepare a list of everything your customers look for in your products. Write down specific examples of how you will discuss each of these items with your customers.

#12

Why Your First Impression Should Never Depend On A Second Effort

How many opportunities do you get to create a favorable first impression? You got it, one and only one. It can be a moment of truth, or if you focus your energy and effort to a positive outcome it can be a magical moment.

Not too many years ago psychologists reported that it took two minutes for a first impression to be formed. Today psychologists report that we have only thirty seconds to create that first impression. A popular business publication, in a recent article, said the decision to hire prospective employees is being made during the first four seconds.

Whether it's four seconds or thirty, there is increasing pressure on the time that's available for launching a positive first impression. Since you can't replay a first impression, it's logical that you get it right the first time.

The old saying, you never get a second chance to make a good first impression, is certainly applicable to your sales efforts. So, what can you do to achieve a first class first impression? Here are some suggestions:

❑ Dress for success...make it clean and pressed.
❑ Walk in like a winner...walk tall.
❑ Wear your best smile...and watch what happens.
❑ Use their names...nothing sounds better.
❑ Begin with a sincere thank you...it shows class.
❑ Focus on their needs...not your product.

There's no way to measure the value of a strong and positive first impression. The best way to have any chance of making a lasting impression with a customer is to focus on making a good first one.

Application...

Make a personalized first impression checklist. Begin by writing it down and follow through by committing it to your pre-call routine.

Nothing succeeds like the appearance of success.

Christopher Lasch

#13

How To Take Charge Of Your Attitude

"How's your attitude?" How would you specifically answer that question if you were asked during a sales training seminar? This is how many participants attending my seminars respond:

> "It's fine."
> "It's okay."
> "I have a positive attitude."
> "My attitude is getting better."
> "It's so so."
> "Mine is really good."

You really have to be there to picture a group of sales people, usually from the same company, answering the attitude question with what amounts to an almost lifeless response in front of their peers.

If the question were changed to, "Do you have a positive attitude?" almost everyone in sales would say "yes." When I ask these same groups, who's in charge of your attitude, the universal response is "I am." Yet, when I ask for the definition or meaning of the word "attitude," the room usually goes quiet. Why doesn't every professional sales representative recognize the real meaning and magnitude of his individual attitude?

An attitude can be defined as your manner, disposition, feeling, position, etc., toward another person. It almost always begins with a thought. Since we control our thoughts, doesn't it follow that we should also control our attitudes? The answer of course is "yes." The challenge is to remove the daily obstacles we face such as the weather, problems at home, rejection, negative thoughts, and anything else that prevents us from projecting a positive attitude.

Imagine every sales call beginning as a picture perfect pond. Also, imagine that you are a rock soon to be tossed into the pond. As this rock (you) is being tossed into the pond, you have the opportunity to choose between creating positive or negative ripples. Which will it be?

As the rock always creates ripples after it hits the pond, every sales representative signals her attitude to customers and prospects at the start of each sales call. It's imperative that you check the following before making a sales call.

❑ Check to see that you're smiling.
❑ Double check your appearance.
❑ Prepare specific sales call objectives.
❑ Visualize positive results.

Your attitude is everything. It can help establish rapport, build confidence, influence results, and insure success only when you fully take charge and become determined to always present your prospects and customers with a first class attitude.

Application...

Think of two ways you can improve your attitude before making a sales call.

> **Happiness is not a station you arrive at, but a manner of traveling.**
>
> **Anonymous**

> **Your attitude, not your aptitude, will determine your altitude.**
>
> **Zig Ziglar**

> **Behold the turtle. He makes progress only when he sticks his neck out.**
>
> **James Bryant Conant**

#14

Was It Good For You Too?

The next time you leave a sales call and begin to reflect on how well it went, ask this question:

"Was it good for you...the customer?"

Too often the sales call post-mortem is evaluated strictly from the seller's perspective. Consider what happens when you plan the sales call with only *your* objectives in mind. You could end up placing a higher priority on your needs. During the actual sales call, the seller will focus on making the sale. Presentations that aren't personalized to specific needs can quickly turn into sales pitches for customers who all seem to look alike.

Take for example a sales rep selling microwave ovens. If he thought all his potential customers looked alike, he might believe they were all buying for the same reason - convenience. Imagine how it would affect his presentations. The same story would be told; the same features and benefits would be explained to everyone. Convenience may be a general reason for buying a microwave oven; however, it doesn't get close to pinpointing specific customer needs. People purchase microwaves to heat up popcorn, to cook bacon, to bake potatoes, to boil water for coffee and tea, to defrost, and even to reheat leftovers just to list a few.

The next time you consider evaluating your sales calls, you may learn more about your skills if you have the courage to ask a few questions.

▲ What qualities do you look for in a professional sales representative?

▲ How could I have made this a better sales call?

▲ What advice would you give me for my next call?

If you owned a restaurant and wanted to give your customers the best dining experience available, wouldn't you instruct your staff to ask all guests the same question. How much more could you learn from every customer if you asked a question similar to "How could we make it better?"

Don't leave a sales call with only your thoughts. Find out if your approach was good for them too.

#15

What Happens When Product Training Stiff-Arms Selling Skills Training?

As a professional sales representative, here are several things you can expect during a training program:

- ✍ more slides than there is time for,
- ✍ product managers (PMs) who think *their* products will sell themselves,
- ✍ little time for questions because PMs have too much to cover,
- ✍ too much talk that could have been committed to writing and read at a later date,
- ✍ an emphasis on the "what" and not the "how,"
- ✍ an assumption that product training insures selling training.

If your company training program looks anything like the above, you may have to rely on your own initiative to map out the appropriate sales strategy for your territory. Before you set out to begin selling any new product, system, or service, be sure you have the answers to the following questions.

Have you mapped out the entire selling process? The steps to the process will lead to the path of success. You must know what it will take to succeed.

Do you know how to professionally prospect for customers? You should know how to use the telephone to make appointments. What you say on the phone should be prepared in advance and committed to writing.

Have you prepared questions to ask that will uncover specific needs for your new product? The questions should focus on getting information and pinpointing ways your product can solve problems.

Have you developed a list of benefits that correspond to the the product's features and specifications? You should have prepared in writing how you will introduce these benefits (transitional statements) to your customers.

Have you anticipated common objections that you'll face and developed reasonable and effective responses for them? Every product has a better chance at being marketable if objections are anticipated and responses are preplanned. Do you know what the typical buying signals are likely to be for this product? You should have considered how you will respond to them.

Have you put the pen to paper and prepared several ways you can ask for the order? Getting the decision can be challenging if you haven't thought specifically about several alternatives in advance.

Have you practiced all of the above to work out the rough edges? Things like setting appointments, asking questions, relating benefits, responding to concerns, and asking for the decision don't come naturally to most professionals. They become easier however, after a lot of preparation. Product knowledge is important. So is preparing to sell.

To improve a company fast, develop people fast.

Andrall E. Pearson

The only companies that grow are those that expect their people to grow, and spend time and money and understanding to help them do it.

William Marsteller

#16

Putting The SPIN
Into Your Sales Effort

If you were asked to divide your sales effort into four parts, how easy would it be? You may never have thought about it. So what's the big deal. The big deal is that for sales reps to be consistently successful we must be consistently thinking about our businesses and how we can grow them.

Let's view your sales effort in this way. There are four major pieces and success means really being good in each piece. They are:

> **S**...Selling
> **P**...Planning
> **I**....Information
> **N**...Networking

Putting the **SPIN** into your business could add big dollars to your commissions, and make a big difference in your performance. If you're open to new ideas, like being challenged and willing to take risks, read on.

Selling - A good sales rep will always start with his customer, and not with his product. Starting with your customer begins with acknowledging that the first step in the buying process is need identification. Selling helps buyers see their needs. There are three principal types of selling that must be mastered. The first is telephone selling which includes qualifying decision makers and making appointments. Next is presentation selling which involves one-on-one meetings along with conference and large group presentations. Finally, there is proposal selling which has the dubious distinction of trying to sell your product for you in your absence. If you're too busy to get smart, you may be too busy to update your selling techniques.

Planning - The critical elements to planning should always include thinking, writing, and doing with the emphasis on the doing. Thinking refers to the quiet time set aside to analyze alternatives and prepare objectives. Writing refers to committing to paper critical thoughts and action plans. If it's not in writing and doesn't have a deadline, it won't get done. Doing refers to the daily actions we take to move progressively closer to our goals. There's a big difference between doing something right and doing the right thing. Being efficient is the former and being effective is the latter.

Information - There are two major components of sales information. First is the information we must find out about our customers. Do you know what their specific needs are? What is their budget? What is their current business situation? What are the trends with your customers' customers? What is their criteria for making a decision? The second component of information relates to how effectively you get your message across to the customer. It includes selling tools, detail sheets, proposals, company brochures, organizational charts with photographs, product samples, and demos when appropriate.

Networking - Years ago networking referred to good old-fashioned talking to people. It now means talking to all the people inside and outside of your company that can help you grow your business. Make a list of everyone in your network. How often do you talk to these people?

Growing your business is easy if you put the right SPIN on it.

Whatever is worth doing at all, is worth doing well.
                                Earl of Chesterfield

Instead of shying away from risks, I attract them, provoke them.
                                Picasso

#17

How To Avoid Turning A
Sales Call Into An Adventure

Next to closing a sale, the thing most salespeople dread is
sounding canned. Salespeople will go out of their way not
to sound like another sales rep. As a matter of fact, it's such
a major concern I think it actually affects the way we
prepare for our sales calls.

Here is a brief list of things professional sales reps could
prepare prior to making a sales call:

> ➪   prepare your objectives,
> ➪   prepare your opening comments,
> ➪   prepare your questions,
> ➪   prepare how you will introduce benefits,
> ➪   prepare your response to common objections,
> ➪   prepare your transition to the close,
> ➪   prepare how you will ask for the decision.

Let's define how we're using the word "prepare." Prepare
means to think and write about what you'll soon be doing in
front of the customer. A lot of training programs try to get
sales reps to use the same lines and responses to specific
customer situations. It's only natural that we don't want to
come across as being plastic and insincere.

Sales people I've observed typically tend not to prepare their comments and questions in advance, instead preferring to respond spontaneously thus avoiding sounding canned. In essence, they treat every call like an adventure. Adventures can be fun, but would you want your dentist or doctor treating you as an "adventure?"

How do customers react to the ways we introduce ourselves, the types of questions we ask, how we introduce benefits, the way we handle objections, and ultimately how we ask for the order if we are always winging it. Customers and prospects often become indifferent and price sensitive because so many sales people don't prepare in advance and use the all too common John Wayne shoot from the lip approach.

Remember...
- ☞ Being prepared is not being canned.
- ☞ Customers can tell how prepared you are.
- ☞ Preparation builds confidence.
- ☞ Preparation allows for personalization.
- ☞ Prior preparation prevents poor performance.

A sales call should not be an unplanned adventure. When you combine preparation with personalization you'll get professionalism, and your sales will take off. The biggest benefit to you is that you'll distinguish yourself from the majority of sales people calling on your customers - thus creating a major personal selling advantage.

Application...

Think and write what you'll say before you say it. Got it?

When an archer misses the mark, he turns and looks for the fault within himself. Failure to hit the bull's-eye is never the fault of the target. To improve your aim - improve yourself.

Gilbert Arland

If you don't know where you're going, you could wind up someplace else.

Yogi Berra

#18

Take A Mulligan

The weekend golfer often views the mulligan as a friend and ally on the pressure packed first tee. For those of you who may never have played golf, a mulligan is an extra shot usually offered and always taken after a terrible golf shot is made, usually on the first tee. Quite literally it's a chance to do it over again. Usually this second shot turns out better than the first. I think it's because most of us rationalize the poor, misplaced, first attempt as a practice shot.

What a great way to think about our sales calls. Imagine all the things that can often go wrong during a call. Things like, but not limited to:

- ❑ the way we fail to adequately plan our specific objectives,
- ❑ botched efforts at establishing rapport,
- ❑ the kinds of questions we ask,
- ❑ our inability to listen,
- ❑ a mishandled objection,
- ❑ our failure to ask for the order at the appropriate time.

Experiencing any of the above can cause us to take a mental sales dive. We sing our song of regret and needlessly carry that baggage around for the rest of the day.

The next time you blow it during a sales call, give yourself a sales mulligan. View the mistake as a practice shot. Taking the mulligan gives you another chance. Reframing the mistake as a practice shot provides a needed boost to your self-confidence, and allows you to continue making calls for the remainder of the day on a more positive note.

As a part of my consulting business, I'll often spend a day in the field travelling with sales representatives to prepare for a personalized sales training program. On one such trip, I was working with the Chicago representative for an environmental lab. Prior to the call she told me her objectives, which included getting the client's reaction to her recently submitted proposal. She added that since this was the first time she would be meeting the client, she wanted to avoid any mention or discussion of a service problem that occurred eight months earlier.

As the call went on, you could see her building rapport and garnering lots of good information from the client. He even complimented her company's past service. This brought an immediate reply which included, "I'm glad to hear you're happy with our service; I thought for sure you'd bring up the problem we had months ago." His expression changed immediately. He said he had forgotten all about that. The next five minutes were spent muddling around the old problem.

She didn't realize it at the time, but as she proceeded to turn the call around to a more positive note, she did it by taking a sales mulligan. She realized her mistake, reframed it as a practice shot, knowing she had more shots left during the call.

When you make a mistake, take a mulligan to feel better.

> **Finish every day and be done with it. You have done what you could. Some blunders and some absurdities no doubt crept in; forget them as soon as you can. Tomorrow is a new day; begin it well and serenely with too high a spirit to be cumbered with your old nonsense. This day is all that is good and fair. It is too dear, with its hopes and invitations, to waste a moment on the yesterdays.**
>
> **Ralph Waldo Emerson**

> **There is always another chance . . . . This thing that we call "failure" is not the falling down, but the staying down.**
>
> **Mary Pickford**

#19

From Crayons To Notebooks

"Once technology is out of the jar, you can't put it back in," said Ervin L. Giaspy. Gone are the days where you could effectively manage a sales territory out of your briefcase and a number of pay telephones. We are indeed approaching the 21st Century and the business of selling is rapidly changing. For example, one large telephone company recently announced plans to take offices away from their sales reps once they are equipped with state-of-the-art notebook computers.

Computers and related technology if used properly can increase selling time, decrease in-basket paper, and effectively manage the increasing flow of information. For example, pagers and portable phones can dramatically improve response time to priority customers. Sales call reports can be sent daily using a modem. Notebook computers make it possible to give customers pricing information, product availability, and order confirmation while you are in their office. Sales forecasts and quotas are being completed on pre-formatted disks that allow sales reps to perform numerous "what if" scenarios to improve planning. Technology has the potential to increase your personal sales production and commissions.

Here are just a few examples of how technology has a positive impact on selling results: easy to prepare proposals; templates for territory promotions and announcements; personalized templates for all customer contacts including records, notes, and lead tracking; calendars; reminder notes; presentations; and even daily "to do" lists.

Three trends for sales technology can be summed up in three words: "more," "compact," and "universal." In the future there will be more options. One example could be sales reps producing their own animated personalized customer presentations, instead of using overhead transparencies to make the same points. Everything related to technology is getting more compact and will continue to get smaller. In the future you're likely to see universal applications of systems and how they are used. As an example, the recent alliance between computer giants Apple and IBM made both systems virtually compatible.

Sales reps out-of-touch with technology could, in the future, find themselves out-of-step with prospective customers.

Traditional thinkers say, "If it isn't broken, don't fix it." But Breakthrough Thinkers say, "Fix it before it breaks."

Gerald Nadler

#20

The Best Dumb Questions

In his newly released book, *Managing For The Future*, Peter Drucker revisits the old idea of managing by walking around. His message for managers forty years ago was to get out of the office and talk to peers and associates. Now he's discouraging that and asking managers to go out and visit customers and ask them lots of dumb questions.

There's a real lesson in these words for salespeople. You have already taken 50% of his advice by being with your customers. The other half won't come so easily if you prefer telling to asking, as so many sales reps do. The key to understanding your customers has more to do with the questions you ask than the answers you have.

What's the implication to a professional sales rep if she can't quickly recite the 15 questions she commonly uses in her presentations? What could it possibly reveal if she needed 10 minutes to think about those questions before she could recall them successfully. Sad but true, it shows a lack of having and using prepared questions. Here are some of my favorite dumb questions. Try them on for size and add your own to the list.

☞ Tell me about your business.

☞ What are your priorities?

☞ What's your criteria for evaluating new products?

☞ What qualities do you want in a sales representative?

☞ How would you like to improve the product you're using?

☞ Describe your responsibilities.

☞ How did you ever get into this business?

☞ How do you define service?

☞ What does quality specifically mean to you?

☞ How will you measure the success of using our product?

☞ What happens when your product lets you down?

☞ What's preventing you from giving us an evaluation?

☞ How are we doing so far?

☞ How can we improve our service?

☞ If you could change one thing about us, what would it be?

Asking questions shows interest, creates understanding, builds rapport, and shortens the selling cycle. If you're not asking enough questions, ask yourself - why not?

#21

Multi-Level Selling Strategies

How well are you staying in touch with your customers and prospects? Not bad, you say. Well, take a closer look. The reference to customers means all types: small, medium, and large. The reference to prospects also refers to small, medium, and large.

Are you giving equal coverage to customers and prospects? Should you be giving them equal coverage? What about large and small accounts, do they deserve equal sales coverage? The two most common ways to interact with customers and prospects is the face-to-face call and the telephone call. Here are some ways to effectively reach your customers and prospects.

FAX - The FAX can be a great communication tool. A high impact message can be added to a creatively designed cover sheet. You can use a FAX to say the proposal is in the mail, to ask for their reaction to your proposal, to confirm a meeting, to answer a question promptly, or to announce a new product offering.

Personal notes - If you're not sending personal notes to inside and outside customers, you are missing out on the most effective way to say thanks, show appreciation, and recognize special achievements. A note comes in a small envelope that is handwritten and stamped. The card is handwritten with a very specific and personalized message. You read it once, maybe twice, and you can't remember the last time you got one. Don't miss the chance to make someone feel real good.

Phone - Be sure you call every small customer on your list at least once a year. A personal call followed up with a handwritten note is far more than most small customers ever get. Keep in touch.

Entertainment - Don't overlook an early breakfast as a way to keep in touch with an important customer or prospect. Tell them you appreciate how busy they are and how they'll benefit from an early morning breakfast. Many of your customers are early morning risers, and would be glad to meet you for breakfast. Check out your customers' parking lots to see how many of them are getting to work before 7:00 A.M.

Letters - Periodically send a short letter introducing something new, or announcing a change in a particular way you're doing business - preferably one that benefits the customer. Your hand signed letter may be sent with additional explanatory information. Inject some of your personality into the letter. Avoid letters that convey *"I'm a form letter."*

Special cards - "Wasn't that a nice touch." That's what they'll say when you send a thoughtful birthday, anniversary, or special occasion card. If you want to be like everyone else, simply send a Christmas card. If you want to gain a small but special advantage over the competition, take a special interest in your customers and their families.

Audio tapes - Did you ever think to send your customers an audio tape? A ten minute tape, recorded in your office and duplicated elsewhere, can be an effective way to reach those hard to reach customers.

Video tapes - If you're willing to think big, you could record and send a video tape. Imagine a ten minute tape that gives you the opportunity to tell some very select customers about your new product. How many people do you know who don't own a VCR?

Newsletters - With the availability of desktop publishing, anyone can inexpensively create and mail newsletters to keep customers and prospects informed.

OPI (other people's information) - If you see an interesting article in a magazine or journal, send a copy with a note to your customers and prospects.

There are many ways to keep in touch. Remember, out of sight, out of mind. Capitalize on these ideas to increase your visibility with customers and prospects.

#22

How To Be UNsuccessful

While there is a long list of characteristics that successful sales reps should want to cultivate, there's a short list of qualities that should be avoided. They include the following:

Unadaptable - in sales, more than any other profession, you can't succeed with rigid thinking, an unwillingness to try new ways, and a selling style rooted to the past. Your future can never be behind you.

Uncommitted - commitment is a powerful word in sales and means a focused effort to improve in key areas. Salespeople have to increase their product knowledge, improve their understanding of customers' requirements, and dedicate themselves to being a team player.

Unemotional - Emerson once said nothing great was ever achieved without enthusiasm. He was right then and he's right now. You must be genuinely excited about your customers' problems, your company, and certainly enthusiastic about the products and services you sell. Your emotions and passion for your work are contagious. Make sure your customers are catching the right thing.

Unhappy - ever notice how unhappy most people look? When you're selling, remember how costly your expressions can be. You can't remove the pain you may have, but you can remove your pained expression. Think of every sales call as a leap onto a stage. Whenever you are in front of a customer, remember it's showtime. We choose our expressions. Make yours a happy one whenever you talk to customers, this includes telephone calls.

Unmotivated - I recently had the opportunity to work with a sales representative who completed a sales training program I presented. During the post-training follow-up, he confided that he was experiencing what he called the January blahs. He showed me his list of goals for the year. Not a single goal had a completion deadline during the first quarter. The quickest way to feeling unmotivated is not having any specific goals. Goals give you purpose while they're getting you motivated.

Unethical - it's really hard to be a little honest, isn't it? There are three reasons why you should always do the right thing. First, you'll immensely increase your personal self esteem. Second, you'll avoid getting caught doing something wrong. Third, you'll sleep better.

Unwelcome - too many salespeople wear out their welcome. They stay too long and talk too much. Say less, listen more, and, as soon as you've achieved your sales call objectives, end the call. You've overstayed your welcome if your customer has to end the call for you.

Remember, to become invaluable you must put more value in everything you do. To achieve selling success you must take out all the little **un's**.

Jim Meisenheimer

Aristotle was asked, "What is the difference
between an educated and an uneducated
man?" He replied, "The same difference as
between being alive and being dead."
Aristotle

Failures either do not know what they want,
or jibe at the price.
W.H. Auden

Failure is the path of least persistence.
Anonymous

No failure in life is as final as the failure to
find out what you do best.
Bernie Weiner

#23

It's Inexcusable To Be
Experienced And Ineffective

Our years of practical sales experience should be a blessing, but often it comes disguised as a curse. Even the adage that hindsight is 20/20 is a misnomer. If hindsight were 20/20, how is it we repeat our mistakes over and over again? Let's examine several qualities of an effective sales representative and the impact experience has on them.

Idea person. If most salespeople, when they first started to sell, put a jelly bean in a jar for every new idea they had during their first year in sales, many could probably spend the rest of their careers emptying the jar with the removal of a jelly bean for each subsequent new idea. Experience seems to inhibit our capacity for new ideas. Keep a log of every new idea you get.

Can-do attitude. Why is it that our experiences sometimes tarnish our shine? The can-do attitude is an emotional thing. There's nothing logical about it at all. When youth and inexperience are joined, they form the partnership called the can-do attitude. As we get older and more experienced, we become more logical. Logic and reason often rule the day. We make decisions and sales calls by logically relying on our filtered experiences without connecting to our emotions. Passion, enthusiasm, and the can-do attitude are the epaulets of winners not just badges for the young and inexperienced. Try injecting upbeat music, inspirational readings, and motivational tapes into your daily routine to recapture your misplaced can-do attitude.

Strategist - Early in my sales career, I remember how I always wanted to be prepared for my sales calls. I recall thinking about what I wanted to achieve during the call, the strategies I would use, and the specific details or tactics that would play a role in making the outcome positive. When I was young and inexperienced, I relied on preparation to see me through. With maturity and more experience came the feeling that they would cushion and almost subsidize my lack of preparation. Soon I discovered that I could wing more calls because of my skills and experience. It wasn't until I started my consulting business, that I once again began to behave like a strategist. I returned to establishing written, clearly defined objectives, strategies, and tactics for all major customers and prospects. I left shooting from the lip to the politicians. Our customers deserve our strategic thinking and planning before we call on them.

You can join a health club for upwards of $2,000 a year. Yes, our bodies need exercise but our minds may need it more. Join a mental gymnastics club. Sound foolish? The alternative can breed ineffectiveness. Books, tapes, video's, seminars, support groups, and professional organizations will add to your experience and effectiveness while giving your mind a great workout. Remember, just because you work out once a year, don't think you're in great shape.

People forget how fast you did a job - but
they remember how well you did it.

Anonymous

It is more than probable that the average
man could, with no injury to his health,
increase his efficiency fifty per cent.

Walter Dill Scott

Effectiveness is doing the right thing,
whereas efficiency is doing things right.

Daniel Stamp

#24

How Do You Spell Success?

If it's possible to spell *relief*...R-O-L-A-I-D-S, then it's more than possible to spell sales *success*...M-E-A-S-U-R-E. It's actually practical and very profitable to measure your way to success.

Superstar sales representatives can tell you exactly how much they've sold, how much is pending, the percent increase in their sales volume, and their relative rank within their sales organization.

At a national sales meeting for a major healthcare distributor, it was customary for the top sales rep to give a brief talk to the sales force during the awards ceremony. Mike had been the top sales rep for three years in a row. So, he was giving his third speech to the group. Dave had finished second this year. He had successfully moved up in his ranking each of the last four years. While Mike was ending his remarks, Dave stood up and in a spirited way that brought the house down said: "Mike, I'm going to get you next year." The following year he did overtake Mike and became the distributor's number one sales rep.

What helped Dave to reach his goal was that he knew exactly where he was and where he wanted to be. The measurement factor can help you chart your course. The measurement principle works in sports, helps students improve their grades, and can significantly increase sales results.

In the morning's paper you can always find the box scores for baseball games. If you're a player, you'll see how many hits, runs, and errors you made, and you see your adjusted batting average. After every game the players get this immediate feedback. You can call it pressure, I call it motivation. However, you can rest assured the impact on performance is generally positive.

Sales reps won't benefit from measuring hits and home runs, but will benefit if they monitor and measure their performance in some of these critical selling parameters.

- Total sales volume
- Total sales dollar increase
- Percent to quota
- Total sales calls per year
- Percent profit margin
- Percent of time allocated to customers and prospects
- Decision ratios (closing)
- Number of presentations
- Number of demonstrations
- Number of sales calls per order
- Relative position to other sales people

Remember, what gets measured gets done. If you want to achieve better results, set goals and constantly measure your performance to the planned objective.

A minute's success pays the failure of years.
Robert Browning

To succeed, jump as quickly at opportunities as you do at conclusions.
Benjamin Franklin

If you wish success in life, make perseverance your bosom friend, experience your wise counselor, caution your elder brother, and hope your guiding genius.
Joseph Addison

#25

Attitude, Platitude, And Gratitude

There are three very important intangibles to consider in every selling situation. A selling situation is defined here as any occasion when sellers are interacting with buyers. It includes telephone and face-to-face communications. Two of the intangibles are positive and are encouraged, while the third is negative and should be avoided.

Number one is your attitude. Attitude is an important part of selling success and may be one of the least understood qualities. A sales person's attitude is very personal and private and affects virtually all aspects of sales. There are six primary attitudes that should be cultivated for successful selling.

1. Your attitude about yourself. Do you see yourself in positive terms and have positive expectations?

2. Your attitude about your products or services. Do you focus on what makes them better and differentiated?

3. Your attitude toward your company. Are you focused on company accomplishments and the quality of people?

4. Your attitude toward planning. Is your calendar organized, and are you setting specific objectives?

5. Your attitude toward customer problems. Do you really view problems as opportunities and welcome them?

6. Your attitude toward customers. Do you see them as your employer and dedicate yourself to serving them?

Attitudes begin with thoughts. So, what are your thoughts about these key attitudes?

Platitudes however are to be avoided like the Bubonic Plague. Platitudes are dull, ordinary comments to everyday situations. How we react in these situations often sets the tone for any potential, future relationship. Three situations which prompt platitudes are when customers refuse to see you, when they are very demanding, and when they say no to your proposal. Instead of serving up traditional platitudes, creatively think about how you can respond unemotionally in these situations.

The third intangible is the one called gratitude. There are so many people who touch and contribute to your selling success why not acknowledge their support. Think about the support and understanding you get from your family. How about the support you receive from your boss and the help you get from your peers? Also, remember the small army of support staff that contributes to your success. Most of all, don't forget your customers. The simplest way to show your gratitude is to say thank you. You can phone, send a note, visit, and even send a small gift. Saying thank you means so much and costs so little, it's a real wonder why it's not done more often. When you say thank you, they'll feel appreciated and want to do even more for you.

Cheerfulness is health; its opposite, melancholy, is disease.
Thomas Chandler Haliburton

'Tis the mind that makes the body rich.
Shakespeare

To be what we are and to become what we are capable of becoming, is the only end of life.
Benedict DeSpiniza

#26

Wanna Be A Know-It-All
Or A Learn-It-All?

While it's true knowledge is power, it's also true that salespeople talk too much. It seems the more we know, the greater is our instinct to blabber on to our prospects and customers.

There are some major differences between a know-it-all (KIA) and a learn-it-all (LIA) sales rep. The KIA from the get-go is armed with answers to questions not even asked. His lead is to sell and tell and he uses the same approach with everyone he sees. He's a pusher type. He pushes his ideas, his products, his solutions, and his attitude. At first, he may appear unlikable, although if given a chance, customers may warm up to him. He treats all customers the same. He has effectively labeled them, and classified them, and knows exactly what they need without ever asking.

The LIA type is totally different in style and effectiveness. She is more likely to ask and listen. She knows that by getting the customer to talk, she's more likely to discover and pinpoint specific customer requirements. She pulls the customer closer because of the genuine interest she has shown. During the first call, she's often viewed more likable than her counterpart the KIA. Because she searches for the unique qualities in every prospect, she's able to personalize her presentation and solutions to individual requirements. Because she has more information, she thinks and acts more strategically.

The LIA type seeks more information in three critical areas: the market served, customer requirements, and the competition. For the LIA the market served, of course, is her territory. The information needed here relates specifically to her territory and not to the market in general. What are her customers' problems? What are the similarities and differences among customers? What are the success factors? She tries to anticipate changes in needs.

Next she has to focus on her customers. It's important to build profiles for each major customer. Do they think in terms of the past, present or future? Do they experience things on an auditory, visual, or kinesthetic basis? Are they focused or do they prefer options and alternatives?

The third critical piece of information is competition. Who are her competitive sales reps? What are their strategies, especially in major accounts? Where are they vulnerable? Why are they successful in her territory?

It's dangerous being a KIA. Too little information creates too many assumptions. Take an interest in your customers by asking questions, learning more, and doing more, and customers will show their appreciation with more business.

It's what you learn after you know it all that counts.

John Wooden

Confess that you were wrong yesterday; it will show that you are wise today.

Anonymous

There is nothing so costly as ignorance.

Horace Mann

It is what we think we know already that often prevents us from learning.

Claude Bernard

#27

Creative "To Do" Lists

Did you ever wonder why so many people are disorganized even after they start writing "to do" lists? Could it be that some people just can't work from lists? The list and prioritize approach isn't suited for everybody. The alternative, especially if you experience things visually, is a to draw a map. I first discovered this application in Joyce Wycoff's book *Mindmapping*.

The basics of mind mapping are covered in chapter 38 in more detail, so all you really need to remember is that your "to do" map is a weekly pictorial representation of all the things you plan to do and all the people you plan to call.

Mapping your "to do" list offers several benefits. If you're a visual person, it's more adaptive to your personal style which means you won't have to bother with linear lists. It's also more fluid and flexible than ordinary lists, which means your more likely to use it and get through more tasks because of your improved organization skills. The use of color and symbols add to the creative process making your "to do" map a vibrant tool for more effectively managing your time.

The creative urge is the demon that will not accept anything second-rate.

Agnes de Mille

Imagination is more important than knowledge.

Albert Einstein

A good beginning makes a good ending.

English Proverb

He who begins many things finishes few.

Italian Proverb

#28

Two Words That Make
Your Benefits Sizzle

If asked, every sales person will acknowledge that customers buy benefits not features. While this is true, many sales reps can't make the distinction, and as a result get features and benefits mixed up, and often make terrible assumptions about the customer's ability to relate a benefit to a feature.

To set the record straight, a feature is a *fact*. For a product, it refers to physical characteristics like color, size, shape, dimensions, and other product specifications. Features are facts and can be considered logical or left brain oriented. Benefits are statements or *illustrations* of how someone specifically gains from the prescribed feature. To be effective, benefits should appeal to the emotions or right brain.

Most sales reps are excellent at reciting the facts about their products. They quote statistics, provide documentary evidence, and often can literally describe product components in minute detail. What they are not good at is appealing to the emotional side of the decision maker. There are several reasons for this. First, most sales reps start their calls by reciting product features. In an attempt to shorten the selling cycle, reps will often start with features and forget the benefits. Second, most product literature and ads are produced in feature format. Last, and perhaps most importantly, we give customers the benefit of the doubt. We assume they know how they'll gain from our product or service.

There's an oxymoron of the highest sales dimension at work here. If we believe that most sales reps don't do an adequate job of presenting benefits, should anyone be surprised that our customers and prospects want to spend more time discussing price.

Price and value are uniquely linked in a bonded relationship. The less emphasis given to value, the greater the desire to discuss price. The inverse is also true.

Selling features is like ordering a plain dinner salad. What really makes it special is the salad dressing. The dressing for every sales presentation is the benefit statements. Facts can be recited but benefits must be sung. Every benefit should tap into the buyer's emotional mind set.

To present benefits effectively and emotionally, think of a stream with a small bridge spanning it. On one side of the bridge is the feature and across the other is the benefit. To get to the benefit you'll need this bridge called a transition. The two best words to introduce a benefit and to heighten its emotional appeal are *which means*. The two words, *which means*, introduce the pending benefit and create the transition from facts to benefits.

For the sales rep, the words *which means* provide added emphasis and let the customer know why he should consider your product. When it refers to exercise, you probably recognize the phrase "no pain - no gain." When it comes to selling "no gain" means "no sale." Spelling out your benefits is one of the easiest ways to make a profitable sale.

> **Sell the benefit, not the feature. People don't buy a newspaper. They buy news.**
> **Anonymous**

> **In the factory we make cosmetics, but in my stores we sell hope.**
> **Charles Revson**

#29

Polaroid Selling

If you've ever used a Polaroid camera, you know the biggest benefit is in being able to see your picture within minutes. It provides instant gratification to the photographer. Imagine what it would be like for a sales rep to take several Polaroid snapshots whenever she made a first sales call on a prospect.

What would you hope to capture with three or four photographs of the prospect and his immediate surroundings? First of all, if you could take pictures on every initial sales call, you really wouldn't have to pay attention to so many details. If post-sales call pictures were available, you could concentrate more on what you're going to say next instead of employing your observational skills.

Let's assume we have our camera in hand and we are able to take pictures, without any adverse reactions from our customer or prospects. If you could only take three pictures what would they be? Only three pictures, so you must be selective. What are the most important things you want to remember after the sales call?

Consider this list and add your own ideas in the space provided.

- ❑ The customer's face
- ❑ Customer's eyes
- ❑ Customer's jewelry and accessories
- ❑ The customer's appearance (clothing)
- ❑ The customer's desk
- ❑ Photographs
- ❑ Awards
- ❑ Status symbols
- ❑ Certificates
- ❑ Reading material
- ❑ Reference books
- ❑ Competitive catalogs
- ❑ Office layout
- ❑ Customer's secretary
- ❑ Customer's notes
- ❑
- ❑
- ❑

We all realize how impractical it is to take pictures during a sales call. What happens when we leave a customer or prospect without capturing these important images? How can we capture these impressions without taking Polaroid's? Each of us has a God given camera in the form of our eyes. How we use them to record our visits, our impressions, and specific details of our customer will often spell the difference between success and failure.

What you see may determine what you sell.

One picture is worth more than ten thousand words.

Chinese Proverb

Treat every customer as if they have a million dollars because they may.

Anonymous

There is only one boss. The customer. And he can fire everybody in the company from the chairman on down, simply by spending his money somewhere else.

Sam Walton

#30

Writing Your Own Ticket

The best way to quickly get from one city to another, especially when there's a lot of miles between them, is to take a plane. Anyone who has flown realizes you can't fly without using an airline ticket. Have you ever really looked closely at an airline ticket? Probably not. That's too bad, because your selling success is almost a sure thing if your sales plan resembles your next airline ticket.

The center piece for every ticket is the destination. Imagine how already poorly managed airlines would function if destinations were omitted from all tickets. There would be total chaos, with ensuing accidents, enraged passengers, and tremendous losses in revenue and life.

For the weary traveller, knowing how to get there is second only in importance to knowing where he's going. How valuable would that prepaid ticket be if the destination didn't have the name of the airline and a specific flight number? Even now, having selected an airline and committing to a particular airline flight number is no guarantee that he'll get there on schedule.

In addition to knowing the destination, airline, and flight number, wouldn't you consider the consequences dire if you failed to have a specific date and time for your flight. Imagine arriving at the airport for your long awaited two week vacation to the Bahamas only to be told your plane left three days earlier and all remaining flights are booked for the next week.

To achieve personal selling success be sure you write your own selling plan (ticket). Here are some steps for making sure your sales plan includes the essentials for your ticket to success.

Do these:

- ❐ Spell out your success in specific terms (goals) - destination.
  You can't "do" goals.
  Action steps show the way and the how.
- ❐ Set deadlines for achieving your goals.
  Make them realistic...but make them.
- ❐ Create a meaningful reward for yourself for every major achievement you accomplish.
- ❐ Detail your plans for achieving success in writing.
  This will help you clarify your goals and you will benefit from seeing them written down.

Ask these questions:

- • What do you want to achieve?

- • Why is it important to you?

- • How will you achieve it?

- What are you willing to sacrifice?

- How many overnight successes did it over night?

> **Before everything else, getting ready is the secret of success.**
>
> **Henry Ford**

> **Good fortune is what happens when opportunity meets with preparation.**
>
> **Thomas Edison**

> **If you don't do your homework, you won't make your free throws.**
>
> **Larry Bird**

Jim Meisenheimer

#31

Hear It Again For The First Time

When I first heard those words, I couldn't believe my ears. Bill Gove, the first president of the National Speakers Association, was working with me on my presentation skills, when he said the words "Hear it again for the first time."

As a sales trainer, it struck me how appropriate it is for sales people to want to periodically review the fundamentals in their pursuit of peak performance. Too often, our training programs, seem like "once in a lifetime occurrences." Instinctively, our guard stiffens and goes up as soon as we recognize any training effort as familiar. Why is that?

My theory has to do with self-esteem. Actually it has to do more with the lack of self-esteem for sales people. How many sales representatives view themselves as professionals in the same vein as professional athletes, actors, lawyers, and doctors? I'll wager not too many. If our perception is one of professionalism, why do we have a problem with committing to the rituals required for professionalism. If we change our perceptions, should we alter our behaviors? Probably.

Instead of being turned off by the familiar aspects and material of many sales training programs, wouldn't it be wonderful to seek out annual renewals to reinforce the things we know and to remind us of the things we may have drifted away from.

Hear it again for the first time. In baseball, the annual spring training ritual held in Florida and Arizona is really a hear it again for the first time opportunity for all players. "All players" refers to those earning seven million dollars and to those making a paltry three-hundred thousand. For a baseball player, what they hear again for the first time includes: exercising, running, fielding, stealing bases, bunting, batting, throwing, and other basics. Sound mundane? Well it is. What is basic is often essential.

Just before Johnny Carson retired there was an article about the departing Doc Severenson, his famed sidekick and band leader. The article talked about how great he was and then there was a single sentence referring to how he practiced the scales every day for two hours. Boring isn't it? Not for a professional. For a professional, it's standard operating procedure. Professionals prepare and practice.

To those at the top of their profession, professional sales offers pride, substantial income, and incredible security. If you buy the concept of professionalism, do you also subscribe to the things that you should be hearing again for the first time? Things like questioning, profiling customers, handling concerns, asking for the decision, communicating, and negotiating?

Hear it again for the first time. That's when the birds sing.

We are what we repeatedly do. Excellence, then, is not an act but a habit.

> Anonymous

Only a mediocre person is always at his best.

> Somerset Maugham

Quality is not an act. It's a habit.

> Aristotle

The chess-board is the world; the pieces are the phenomena of the universe; the rules of the game are what we call laws of Nature.

> Thomas Henry Huxley

#32

What Color Is Your Customer?

If we could go back to the time of Hippocrates, we would learn that he was the first person to recognize that people can be classified into four personality groups.

Today there are many psychological instruments that measure and analyze personality. Most of them are derived from Hippocrates' theory and many are as complicated as they are instructive.

Imagine all people classified as one of four colors. Each color has distinctive characteristics from the others. How would you benefit from a clear understanding of each color as we approach and interact with potential customers? What's the implication when you are reminded that people often like people most like themselves?

The following is a brief list of personal qualities.
- Which ones are most like you?
- Which qualities most closely resemble your customers?
- How can the quality of communication and negotiation be improved with an increased awareness of personality traits?

	Red	**Green**	**Yellow**	**Blue**
Type	Organizer	Director	Controller	Planner
Time	Now	Now	Past	Future
Asks	What	Who	How	Why
Style	Doer	Talker	Guardian	Thinker
Focus	Task	People	Task	People
Interaction	Direct	Direct	Indirect	Indirect
Priority	Building	Selling	Scheduling	Planning
Likes to	Solve problems	Persuade	Do detail	Innovate
Prefers	Seeing it finished	Motivating	Numbers	Ideas

"The above chart adapted and used with permission of Birkman and Associates, 1993."

Which color is most like you? Hard to figure out? What's your time orientation - now, past, or the future? Which questions are you most likely to ask - what, who, how, or why? Do you tend to focus more on people (like greens and blues) or more on tasks (like reds and yellows)? Do you prefer to communicate with people directly, or do you feel more comfortable communicating indirectly?

Whichever color you relate to, please recognize that your customers are very likely to be a different color with different perspectives. Don't settle for just finding out which products and prices are important to your customers. Learn as much as you can about how they think, feel, and react to different situations. That may be easy to say and very hard to do. Where should you begin? Begin with a self-assessment. Learn as much as you can about your own personality characteristics and how you are different from others. Make it a daily habit to become more observant around people. A good way to reinforce this practice is to take notes. Write down key observations about your customers. This new habit will pay big dividends now and later.

Remember, sometimes your customers say **no** because you really don't **know** them. Professional sales representatives can't afford to be "color blind."

Special note: If you're interested in finding out more about your "color" call Jim Meisenheimer (708) 680-7880. The above information is based on the Birkman Method, which has successfully profiled over 750,000 people during the last 40 years.

> **You can make more friends in two months by becoming interested in other people than you can in two years by trying to get people interested in you.**
>
> Dale Carnegie

#33

Are Your Customers Seeing Red?

Whenever you have the opportunity to send a proposal to a customer or prospect don't overlook the benefit of doing it in color. Too many sales reps consider the formal proposal simply a necessary follow-up to a face-to-face sales presentation. Actually, the proposal can take on added dimensions and value if it's prepared properly.

Consider these important benefits.

The proposal:

- offers a written summary of benefits,
- gets passed around to key people,
- reinforces key points in your absence,
- will be compared to others that are submitted,
- has tremendous appeal to people who are very visual.

The written proposal is a powerful selling tool if it's used correctly. Sending your customer a written follow-up is not enough. Imagine a sales call lasting 45 minutes in which the customer didn't take any notes. The meeting goes well and you feel you did a good job of establishing rapport and discovering needs. The customer wants some time to consider your product. You leave the account feeling there is a high probability of getting the order. Your first reaction is to send a brief note recapping the meeting; you include a summary of your capabilities and the pricing information. If you're up against two or three competitors, consider preparing and sending a blockbuster proposal.

Proposals, if prepared professionally, can be partners in selling. If they are really good, they can be extraordinary partners. The two most important elements of a proposal are substance and style. First the substance. Be sure your proposal includes a summary of objectives, company capabilities, product features and benefits, an organization chart, key contact information including phone numbers and addresses, FAX numbers, and naturally your pricing information.

Remember, your substance is 50% of the proposal. The other 50% is how it looks, its style. Here are several high impact suggestions. Prepare a professional cover sheet that includes the key contact's name and company name - it's a very nice personal touch. Also, if you're sending more than ten pages consider a spiral binding. The next suggestion offers high value and high impact. The page immediately preceding the pricing page should be your proposal benefits page. Place as many facts with related benefits on this page as you can. Label the page BENEFITS. If you have the capability and want an even greater impact, list all the benefits in red. You'll need a color printer to do this.

A sales rep who attended one of my seminars credits this benefits page in getting an order for $500,000. To increase the value of your proposal make sure your customers are seeing your benefits in red.

To create is to think more efficiently.

Jean Renoir

Imagination means letting the birds in one's head out of their cages and watching them fly up in the air.

Gerald Brenan

There is nothing mysterious about originality. Nothing fantastic. Originality is merely the step beyond.

Louis Danz

#34

Discombobulated?

Before you throw up your hands and say, "Who, me?" remember, it's only natural to occasionally feel anxious, stressed, and even frustrated. The key word is occasionally.

There's an old saying that says a problem defined is a problem half solved. There are several tell-tale signs which may serve as a yellow warning light for you.

Pressed for time - In the complex, quick-paced world we work in, it's often impossible to get everything accomplished on a daily basis. Our busy schedules can often serve us a double whammy. We schedule too much. We start with the easy things first in order to get them out of the way. Since we can't get everything done, we may wind up carrying over high priority items to the next day adding to the pressure because we failed to get the important things done. Remedy - try to schedule your priorities instead of prioritizing your schedule. Remember first things first, focus on what's important.

At your wits end - Did you ever feel that you had an order locked up, only to learn on the next call that someone with a lot of authority just tossed in a left-handed monkey wrench? You were already planning how to spend your commissions.

Now it seems like you're being asked to go back to step one. You might feel like screaming or experience an ordinary sinking feeling. Oftentimes, the situation isn't to blame, we are. Remedy - remember the difference between the trees and the forest. Take a step backward to move forward. Distance increases your perspective. It doesn't diminish it. Try using pencil and paper to sketch the situation and alternatives for resolving it. There's a real benefit in seeing your problem and options on paper.

Boxed, blocked and caged - There's only one roadblock to closing the deal. From the customer's perspective it's deserved; from your point-of-view it's the last straw and could be a deal-breaker. Examples of what the customer is looking for might include: a request that you beat a competitor's price, a concession in terms and conditions, or even a request for a costly product modification. If your experience tells you there's no way out, remember there was a way in. Remedy - creativity and innovation. Make a list of 12 benefits. Make another list that includes five trades you can make with the customer, i.e., if you do this, we'll do this. Just because it feels like your trapped in a cage, don't assume the doors are locked. Shake up your thinking, and you'll stir up the results.

Feeling discombobulated goes with every sales position. Anticipate it and think creatively about how to deal with it when it pays you a visit. It's really an opportunity to deal with adversity and we all know how it feels to triumph over adversity.

No pessimist ever won a battle.
                              Dwight Eisenhower

You work hard and you're finally on Easy Street; then you discover there's no parking.
                              Anonymous

The bold are helpless without cleverness.
                              Euripides

You may be disappointed if you fail, but you are doomed if you don't try.
                              Beverly Sills

#35

Win, Place, Or Show?

When it comes to getting an order, there's only one thing worse than getting skunked; it's coming in second or third because of a failed effort that just misses the mark. From the customer's perspective you've come up short. From your own point of view, you may rationalize that the customer had unreasonable expectations.

It's one thing to get skunked. It's quite another not to get the winner's nod because you missed doing something small.

Here are five ways to beat *out* the competition:

Outbid - The way to outbid the competition is not to lower your price, but to raise your value. Too often, requests for quotations are handled in a very vanilla way. The focus is often on your pricing and terms. The way to outbid the competition is to load up the proposal with features and benefits. Place them on a separate page preceding your pricing page. Now, they won't see your price until they've seen your benefits.

Outdistance - There is no easy way to go the extra mile. If it was easy, everyone would do it. By doing things that require extra work and effort you will, in time, differentiate yourself from your competitors.

Outlast - Woody Allen once remarked that life was 90% just showing up. While that may not be totally true in sales, far too many sales reps give up too early. We run from resistance. We can't bear to hear the rejection in the word "no." So we simply move on. Don't quit so soon. Try again. Call again. Close again. Sometimes the last person in is the rep who has called the most and stayed the longest. Remember, don't ever give up. Never think never.

Outfox - I've heard from many sources, that we should try to think like the customer. Well we should. We should also think like our competitors, if we want to outfox them, especially in a very competitive situation. Ask yourself how the competition has reacted in the past, who is likely to get involved, why would they consider certain options, and what are their objectives.

Out-of-step - The quickest way to get side-tracked with your customers is to start with your products instead of their problems. Customers buy solutions to problems. They seldom purchase just products. How specific are the problems you've identified? Specific customer problems demand personalized solutions. To get in step with your customers, align yourself with their needs. You're either in step or out-of-step. Get it?

If you want to finish third, show your customers how little you offer. If you want to finish a close second, place your extra effort on the back burner. If you want to win, strive to outbid, outdistance, outlast, and outfox your competitors.

The difference between a successful person and others is not a lack of strength, not in a lack of knowledge, but rather in a lack of will.

Vincent T. Lombardi

If you don't invest very much, then defeat doesn't hurt very much and winning is not very exciting.

Dick Vermeil

A winner . . . knows how much he still has to learn, even when he is considered an expert by others. A loser . . . wants to be considered an expert by others, before he has even learned enough to know how little he knows.

Sydney Harris

#36

How To Become *In*valuable

Did you ever wonder why some words mean more than others? For example, the word "value." By itself it has one meaning. Add the suffix "less" and it doesn't mean as much. With the prefix *"in "* added to the word "valuable" its meaning changes dramatically.

Sales people seek to increase the value of their products and services without always being successful. If you want to become invaluable, you must first increase your value. You do it by putting something *in* to the existing value.

Here are fourteen things you can do to substantially increase your value to your customers.

1. Do lots of little things.
There's an old saying that little things mean a lot. In sales it's untrue. Remember, the little things are paramount. A handwritten personal note, a birthday card, a warm and sincere thank you after an order has been received, are several examples of little touches that often mean a lot. Remember that business is people.

2. Set an example.
Are you walking your talk? When it comes to the competition, do you set the standard for punctuality, reliability, knowledge, resourcefulness, and problem-solving? The adage that your actions speak louder than your words sums it up.

3. Be positive.
Your attitude casts a big shadow. Is it the one you want it to have? Acting positively is a function of thinking positively. The only way to act positively is to constantly fill your head with positive thoughts. A quick way to check your attitude is to observe your reflection of the person you're with.

4. Tell customers what you are doing.
Be sure you share the reasons regarding how and why you do things. Don't ever assume that your customers know too much about you, your products, or your company. A well informed customer is a loyal one. This goes double for bad news. If you're going miss a delivery schedule, call them with the reasons and the revised schedule. They'll appreciate your directness.

5. Keep asking questions.
It's the only road to discovery. Ignorance is never bliss. Questions show your interest; and after lots of good questions, you'll end up knowing an awful lot about your customer. The more you know about your customers, the easier it'll be to personalize your solutions using your products. Remember the goal is not to sound like everybody else.

6. Ask, how are we doing?
Don't assume everything is going according to the customer's expectations. Always keep in mind that your customer is someone else's prospect. Make certain you keep well informed on all areas of dissatisfaction, no matter how small.

7. Ask, how can we do it better?
If you like the last question, you should love this one. This is the essence of letting your customers drive the momentum of your business. Asking about the little things that would make your products and services better, telegraphs to your customer that you care and value his input. If you know how he would make it better before the competition does, you'll never lose the loyalty of your customer.

8. Listen carefully.
There are two distinct benefits for sales reps who listen to their customers. First, you'll be very popular with them. Second, you'll probably learn something you didn't know. Listening increases knowledge and builds rapport quicker than any other approach.

9. Write right.
Your writing tells your story when you're not there. There are three things to consider before penning that memo or customer letter. First, think about what you want to say before you write the first word. Develop your focus. Second, say it with headlines, visuals, and color. Today, more than ever, people are responding to visual presentations. Third, write as if you're writing a telegram and paying for each word. Remember, less is more with today's written communication.

10. Speak right.

For people who sell and communicate, the words we use are the craft we have to master. Careless language is no better than a misspelled word. Remember the importance of impact; try to grab your audience at the very beginning of your talk or presentation. To be really effective and memorable, focus on a strong opening and a memorable closing. We are judged not only by what we say, but increasingly by how we say it. Think of the world as your stage.

11. Think platinum.

The golden rule created during Biblical times shouldn't be forgotten as much as it should be modified for today's business environment. The golden rule says we should treat people the way we want to be treated. In sales, that unfortunately puts the focus on us rather than on the customer where it should be. The platinum rule simply says to treat people the way they want to be treated. Apply that to your customers and watch sales soar.

12. Empower those on whom you rely.

Salespeople rely on customer service personnel, product managers, shipping clerks, manufacturing representatives, accounts receivable staff, research and development departments, and upper management to adequately serve customers. Too many sales reps try to shield their customers from people at the home office under the banner of "Nobody knows my customers like I do." Give others in your organization an opportunity to serve your customers and watch them rise to the occasion. Oftentimes, this will free you up to sell more.

13. Award "Little Oscar's."
Recognize that recognition motivates. Most people can count on recognition for every home run they hit. For most of us there are lots of innings between home runs. Folks are starving for recognition. Even in its simplest form, it packs a tremendous wallop. Handwritten notes work great, phone calls, flowers, a bottle of wine, a lunch or dinner, and even a very warm and sincere thank you all create recognition.

14. Keep fixing it.
Assume it's always broken. Don't settle for the past. Keep your eye on the future. Seek small, continuous improvements in everything you do. Anticipation and change are the buzz words for the 1990's.

You determine your value.

> **The secret of business is to know something that nobody else knows.**
> **Aristotle Onassis**

#37

To Do Or Not To Do?

Sometimes, like our dreams, the real world isn't what it seems. For example, most sales people when asked, say they are organized. A majority will cite their goal orientation as supporting evidence. Now for the gap between perception and reality. A 1991 time management survey showed that 86% of business people consider themselves to be goal oriented, while only 46% maintained a daily "to do" list.

Before listing the virtues and benefits of writing a daily "to do" list, here are some of the most compelling reasons for not doing one.

- It's in my head.
- It keeps changing.
- There's not enough time.
- The list is too big.
- I'm too spontaneous.
- What if I don't get the list done.
- I don't want to commit to doing it.

Does this sound at all familiar? It should, since it represents the response of most salespeople. Peter Drucker said ". . . simplicity works best, but what is simple is never easy."

What could be easier than making a list every day of the things you want to get done? The answer, of course, is "nothing." Making lists is so easy and uncomplicated that we are prone to minimizing their importance.

There are three compelling essentials to having an effective "to do" list. First, your list must be in writing. Writing commands commitment. It's the starting point. Second, and very important, is the requirement that all items on your list be prioritized in some way. Either an alpha or numeric system works best. Remember, a list without priorities usually doesn't get done. Finally, you should make a list every day. The habit, to be maintained, must be a daily one. Don't outsmart yourself by skipping weekends.

Here are the benefits:

① You'll have a map for each day.
② You'll always be focused on priorities.
③ You'll have a true sense of accomplishment.
④ You won't get bogged down with little things.
⑤ Your energy will develop passionate purpose.
⑥ You'll be able to see what needs doing.
⑦ You'll achieve more in less time.
⑧ You'll be in charge and in control.

Now compare this list to the list of reasons not to make a "to do" list. You'll see that the benefits actually fight the potential problems. Keeping a "to do" list can make you more effective. You'll be better focused so that you can respond quickly and spontaneously. "To do" lists help you see where you're going so that you can be ready when you get there.

Get smart. Write a "to do" list. Prioritize it. Do it every day. You'll realize very quickly what a difference a list makes.

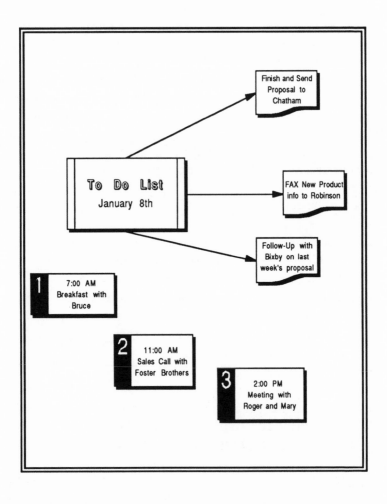

#38

Mapping Your Way To Success

The easiest way to get from one place to another is to use a road map. The closest most sales people get to maps is their car's glove compartment. Even then it's usually a reluctant sales rep who reaches for his map when he's lost. It's usually because of instinct and ego. Instinct, because we really feel we know where we are and where we are going. Ego, because we can't bring ourselves to do it the easy way; our pride forces us to drive around in circles until we eventually, though late, reach our destination.

Before I begin describing the advantages of sales mapping, let's review the common characteristics of maps in general.

- ❏ They are written.
- ❏ They are in color.
- ❏ They use symbols and legends.
- ❏ They use few words.
- ❏ They are very clear and concise.
- ❏ They show the way.

Imagine a mythical sales manager asking you what's going on in a particular account. Also imagine that he asked to see a picture of your plans. How specifically would you respond? Would you be able to respond? Would you immediately wonder why he wants to see it? Wouldn't it be easier to simply tell him about it?

There's an old adage that says "a picture is worth a thousand words." Did you ever wonder why? I did and that's why I recommend sales mapping.

The most important things in life are in writing. Mortgages, wills, checks, letters, and even speeches. Instead of adding reams of paper to your already out-of-control files, why not consider drawing a map. Your sales map can pictorially describe your plan of action for a particular account. If the idea catches on, you may also way to prepare a map of your territory plan. Here's how to do it.

- ✍ Start with a central point or theme.
- ✍ Be imaginative. Use crayons for color.
- ✍ Be concise. Use one word ideas.
- ✍ Use arrows, lines, and boxes to connect points.
- ✍ Focus on what you want to achieve.
- ✍ Add sub-points on how you plan to achieve your goals.
- ✍ Be creative and innovative.
- ✍ Map out your account plan on one page.
- ✍ Be sure your map "shows the way."

Imagine having a picture of your game plan for all major accounts. Thinking about your plans is always step one. Committing them to writing should be step two. Step three could be a creative account map that graphically shows your objectives, strategies, and tactics. Your map should also show how decisions are made, how the customer will measure success, and what the main priorities are.

The dictionary defines a map as a plan, outline, and diagram. Success in selling never comes easy. It will, however, be easier to succeed if you have a plan, outline, and diagram of your selling game plan. The purpose of your map is to help you get there quicker.

Remember...your map will always show the road to success.

Mapping Resources:

Use Both Sides Of Your Brain, Tony Buzan, 1989, Plume.

Mind mapping, Joyce Wycoff, 1991, Berkley.

Mapping Inner Space, Nancy Margulies, 1991, Zephyr.

Inspiration, software for the Macintosh by Inspiration Software, Inc.

The map on the following page was created using Inspiration software.

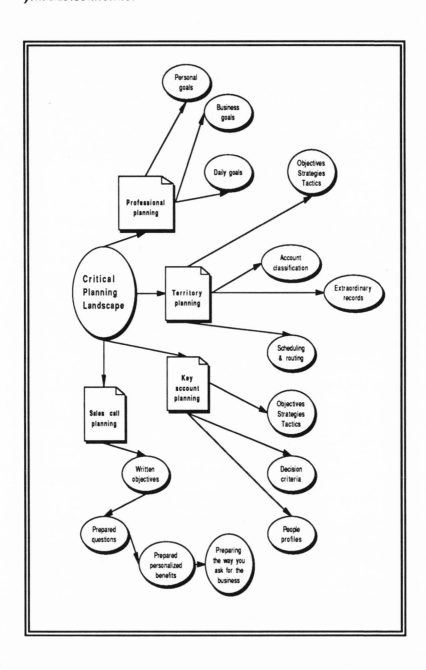

#39

Forget Closing

According to a recent study, a majority of all sales reps never ask for the business. This 1990 survey indicated that 62% of all sales reps never attempt to close. Considering that's what salespeople get paid to do, doesn't that seem like a high number? It sure does, and it's costing sales reps and their respective companies millions of dollars in annual sales, commissions, and productivity.

I have a theory regarding why so few sales reps are bold enough to close. How many of us would enjoy going to a restaurant if we knew it would be our last supper? Who among us would look forward to taking a cruise on a sinking ship? How would you like to adopt a dog named Rabid? None of these are especially appealing, and are made so by the key descriptive words and their implication for us.

There is a time during every attempted sale when it's appropriate and necessary to ask for the order. What isn't as attractive is the thought of closing. The reason is perfectly clear. The word "close" doesn't describe the action that is required. If you doubt this, look up the word "closing" in your dictionary. The word has many meanings and most of them aren't very positive.

Here's a sampling.

- ➪ to terminate
- ➪ to dispose of
- ➪ to grapple
- ➪ to stop
- ➪ to end
- ➪ to block
- ➪ to suspend
- ➪ to liquidate

How many of you are trying to terminate, liquidate, and block your prospective customers? Read on. You can also:

- ➡ close-in . . . . capture or attack,
- ➡ close-out . . . . reduce our price,
- ➡ close-down . . . . terminate,
- ➡ close-call . . . . narrowly escape.

I don't know who invented the word "close" and applied it to the end of the selling process, but I can guess it was done in another century. No one wants to be "closed." I don't, and I suspect you don't. One of the ways to improve our sales performance is to change the way we refer to the last step in the professional selling process.

Once we have identified specific customer needs, presented our solutions, and handled all concerns, we have every right to proceed to the next step. How we view it and what we call it may have a dramatic impact on our results.

Forget the close. Ask for the order, ask for the business, or just try to get "a let's do it today" decision.

#40

That Was Then . . . This Is Now

Telephone booths . . . car phones, cellular phones.
Operators . . . touch tone, voice mail.
Pen . . . word processor.
Post Office . . . Federal Express.
Federal Express . . . The FAX.
Demo equipment . . . Video Presentations.
File folders . . . account contact management
software.
Overhead transparencies (B&W) . . .
computerized graphics.
Selling products . . . pinpointing customers' needs.
More of the same . . . taking risks, breaking what isn't
broken.
Eight layers of management . . . flatter organizations.
Face-to-face selling . . . telemarketing.
Call the office . . . boot up the notebook.
Quota games . . . software - "what-if' scenarios.
Keeping track . . . lead management software.
Trade show selling . . . target based selling.
14 MPG . . . 32 MPG and 50MPG.
Staying for the gold watch . . . watching for the
golden opportunity.
Commanders as managers . . . managers as coaches.
Mass marketing . . . niche marketing.

Telling and selling . . . asking and listening.
Selling the buyer . . . buyers negotiating to win.
Making the sale . . . satisfying the customer.
Start with your product . . . start with your customer.
"Here I am" . . . "there you are."
They'll buy what we make . . . we make what they need.
Lucky Strikes . . . Nicaret gum.
Us versus them . . . we're in this together.
No time to learn . . . classroom in the car.
Doing things right . . . doing the right things.
Calendars . . . time systems.
Prioritizing schedules . . . scheduling priorities.
Out of practice . . . role playing.
Hotel bars . . . hotel health clubs.
Porterhouse . . . Mahi Mahi.
Out of focus . . . out of work.
Marginal service . . . out of business.
Productivity . . . profitability and "relatability."
Strategic planning . . . strategic vision.
Long lunches . . . early breakfasts.
Barbershop shave . . . tanning salon.
Prince tennis rackets . . . Big Bertha golf clubs.
Mainframe computers . . . power notebooks.
Know the customer . . . know the customer's customer.
Aston Martin . . . Dodge Viper.
Experience means a lot . . . training means more.
Meetings . . . meetings interrupted by meetings.
Floppy disks . . . gigabytes on a credit card.
Negotiating seminars . . . negotiating software.
Print advertisements . . . ads on disks, in magazines.
Thirty-something . . . twenty-something, thirteeners.

The past is a foreign country; they do things differently there.

Leslie Poles Hartley

Progress is impossible without change, and those who cannot change their minds cannot change anything.

George Bernard Shaw

When you're through changing, you're through.

Bruce Barton

#41

Beyond The Valley Of Rejection

Have you ever seen a one-sided valley? Probably not. Every valley has at least one side going down and another headed up. If you can imagine a valley as the place where all of the "no sales" reside, it would be noteworthy to develop the right perspective and attitude regarding the slopes to and from.

Since selling success is never a given and certainly not an absolute, most sales reps can expect to meet with occasional rejection and "no sales." This is the slope that leads to the valley of "no sales." Unlike the Grand Canyon, the valley of rejection doesn't have to be deep and wide.

The captivating element of facing rejection is the unique opportunity it presents. Few of us question how and why we succeed. Facing rejection and encountering "no sales" along the way yields a positive learning opportunity for all professional sales representatives.

Asking the following questions will help sales people out of the valley.

      ☞   Is there anything I can do differently?

ᴄᴐ   Am I truly focused on my customers' needs?

ᴄᴐ   How can I show more value in our benefits ?

ᴄᴐ   How positive are my attitude and expectations?

Every valley, especially in sales, creates an incredible opportunity for us to turn our performance around. We do it by being better prepared, more focused, more positive, and more enthusiastic about our work.

In the work I do, primarily sales training seminars and workshops, I rely a lot on my local PIP printer. I can count on Mark to do a good job on my newsletter and training materials. I remember asking Mark how his business was one day in August 1991. He told me it was slow, because of summer vacations, and he wished he had more work, especially since he just added a full-time assistant. About a week later I stopped by around noon, and asked if he could complete my order for three different workbooks by early the next morning. He assured me it would get done. When I got back to my office 45 minutes later, there was a FAX from Mark saying my entire order was ready. Even when his own business was soft, he focused on my needs and gave extra service. Mark's business has been really good lately.

Every valley, especially in sales, creates an incredible opportunity for us to refocus our performance. We do it by preparing more carefully, becoming more focused, giving more service, staying positive, and being more enthusiastic about our work. We can learn from the valleys and should recognize that it's up to us to climb the peaks to success.

We are all, it seems, saving ourselves for the Senior Prom. But many of us forget that somewhere along the way we must learn to dance.

Alan Harrington

For all your days prepare, and meet them all alike. When you are the anvil, bear. When you are the hammer, strike.

Edwin Markham

There's a story told about Henry Ford who was asked by an insurance agent why he had never received any of Ford's business. Replied Ford, "You never asked me."

#42

How Winners Win

Have you ever thought about the margin of victory in America's greatest sporting events? In events like the Olympics, the Kentucky Derby, the Indianapolis 500, the Masters' Golf Tournament, and the Superbowl, there is very little difference that separates first place from second.

In the Olympics it could be .01 seconds; in the Kentucky Derby, it could be a nose; a tire change in the Indy 500; one golf shot over 72 holes of golf in the Masters'; or perhaps a last second field goal to win the Superbowl. How much extra effort would it take to be a fraction better than the competition?

You can safely assume that most winners strive to do a lot of things 1% better than everyone else. The little things add up; and the more of them you perform better than your peers and your competition, the more likely you are to finish in the winner's circle.

Winners like to win. You can also say winners don't like losing. Which one is a greater motivator depends on the individual person. Rest assured they do behave differently. They don't focus on the ordinary. They concentrate on the *extra*ordinary. Here are some of the things winners do more of to win.

- ⇔ They know specifically what they want.
- ⇔ They commit to doing it...it becomes a priority.
- ⇔ They make it a habit.
- ⇔ They form habits others don't.
- ⇔ They know an extra effort can mean 1st place.
- ⇔ They know winning isn't a destination.
- ⇔ They know how to get up when knocked down.
- ⇔ They know hard work often spells success.

There is nothing mysterious about winning, just ask any winner. For them the real mystique is wrapped around losing. People who never win, shouldn't think of themselves as winners. To be a winner you simply have to win.

Application...

What winning initiatives can you make in your business to become more of a winner? Be specific and commit your ideas to writing.

To win without risk is to triumph without glory.
Corneille

A winner is someone who sets his goals, commits himself to those goals, and then pursues his goals with all the ability given him.

Anonymous

The Winner - is always part of the answer;
The Loser - is always part of the problem;
The Winner - always has a program;
The Loser - always has an excuse;
The Winner - says "Let me do it for you;"
The Loser - says "That's not my job;"
The Winner - sees an answer for every problem;
The Loser - sees a problem for every answer;
The Winner - sees a green near every sand trap;
The Loser - sees two or three sand traps near every green;
The Winner - says, "It may be difficult but it's possible;"
The Loser - says, "It may be possible but it's too difficult."
Be A Winner

Anonymous

#43

Your Three Minutes Are Up

The telephone is an important business tool, right? Wrong. Have you ever listened to a group of sales representatives using a bank of hotel telephones trying to schedule appointments? Very few will demonstrate professionalism and the ability to get to the job at hand: i.e., make the appointment.

Today, we're surrounded by telephones including car phones, portable phones, and cellular models. Sales professionals should use the phone to make appointments, confirm demonstrations, follow-up on proposals, and occasionally to obtain commitment.

One of the toughest calls to make is to a prospect you want to see. There are so many things that can foul up the best of efforts including an overly talkative sales rep. While traveling with a sales rep, I spent 15 minutes listening to him detail products over the phone to a person who didn't have time to see us. The buyer's office was no more than 20 yards from the phone the rep was using. In this case the sales rep had forgotten the original purpose of the phone call.

Like so many other reps he literally talked himself out of the appointment.

The two most important steps to making successful appointment calls are these.

1. Have a specific objective and date in mind.
2. Prepare what you say before you say it.

Having a specific objective in mind and in writing will often create a smoother start to your call. Instead of beginning with trite comments like "I'm going to be in your area" or "I wanted to come by to introduce myself," you'll be able to confidently say "I'm calling to arrange," I'm calling to set-up," I'm calling to discuss," etc.

Being prepared is a professional necessity when making appointment calls. First of all, if you're not prepared, you'll sound like it and, even more disturbing, you'll sound like the vast majority of all business people who only think about what they're going to say a nanosecond before its said.

Here are the four basic steps to an appointment call.

1. The greeting. Keep it simple. Speak slowly.
2. The introduction. You and your company.
3. Create interest. A key benefit or question works.
4. Ask for the appointment - as soon as possible.

Making appointments by telephone isn't very complicated if you're prepared. Your preparation will *telegraph* your professionalism. Record yourself. Listen to what your customers hear. If it doesn't sound good to you, how can it possibly sound professional to them?

> **Speech is conveniently located midway between thought, and action, where it often substitutes for both.**
>
> **John Andrew Holmes**

> **Be sure your brain is in gear before engaging your mouth.**
>
> **Anonymous**

#44

The Best 15 Minutes Of
Every Selling Day

Imagine you are working with your sales manager and as you recap the daily schedule for him, he asks one or more of these questions.

- ▶ What's the purpose of the sales call?
- ▶ What do you want to accomplish here today?
- ▶ Why are we making this call?
- ▶ What's the reason for the call?
- ▶ What's the primary sales objective for this call?

How would you respond? Would your response include vague and general comments such as:

- ▶ to make a sale,
- ▶ to introduce a product,
- ▶ to demonstrate a product,
- ▶ to do a review,
- ▶ to find out about the customer's needs.

Or would you respond with very specific sales call objectives that are so specific they could pass through an eye of a needle? There are several key advantages to preparing specific sales call objectives for every sales call. But first, when should you plan these objectives? There's no one good time; however, the best planners always try to set aside the same time each day to map out their objectives and strategies.

You may want to devote fifteen minutes at the end of each day preparing the objectives for the next day. Some reps prefer to do it the evening before, and still others like to do it early in the morning.

How specific should you be when planning your sales call objectives? Consider this: how specific would you want to be if you knew there was a very high correlation between specific objectives and desired results. When you plan exactly what you want to achieve during the sales call, you become incredibly focused and so does the customer.

Here are **five** reasons why you should spend at least fifteen minutes every day planning specific sales call objectives.

1. You'll achieve "definition of purpose."
2. The objective will direct and guide the call.
3. The customer will know why you're there.
4. Your focused efforts will save wasted time.
5. You'll be able to measure results on every call.

The better your plan, the better your results will be. If you'll invest fifteen minutes every sales day to setting specific call objectives, you will turbo-charge your selling effort and dramatically improve your performance.

Remember...
It takes the will to prepare to develop the will to win.

The time which we have at our disposal every day is elastic; the passions that we feel expand it; those that we inspire contract it; and habit fills up what remains.

Anonymous

Time is the scarcest resource and, unless it is managed, nothing else can be managed.

Peter Drucker

Why kill time when one can employ it?

French proverb

The only person to succeed while horsing around is a bookie.

Bob Murphy

#45

Lighten Up . . . For Pete's Sake

In February 1991, two days after Valentine's day, I was scheduled to fly from Atlanta to Dallas to conduct a two-day sales training seminar. I had just completed a two-day workshop sponsored by the National Speakers Association. The workshop was terrific with lots of new ideas and great speakers who shared their wit and wisdom. I checked out of the hotel around 1:00 P.M., and took a taxi to Atlanta's airport. Since I was three hours early for my scheduled departure, I asked about an earlier flight.

The American Airlines agent looked up and said she had room on a flight departing Gate D9 at 1:52 P.M. If I hurried I could make it. With so little time, she told me I had to check my garment bag at the gate. She also said I would have to hurry. Since I always carry my notebook computer, I was expecting to get stopped at the airport security counter. My bags made it through security; but, for some unknown reason, I didn't and proceeded to set off the alarm. A little out of breath and very anxious about the time, I emptied my pockets and went through the check point again, only to set off the alarm once more. The security agent waved over another agent who proceeded to examine me body part by body part. I did what some of us would do and blamed the security person for the delay and for possibly missing my flight.

It's funny how that works. Something in my possession set off the alarm, and I blamed someone else who was only doing his job. If I were getting ready to make a sales call, imagine the frame of mind I would have been in. I wish I could go back and apologize to that security man. I'm sure I didn't contribute anything positive to his day.

What's the point to all this? The point is that many of us are wound up so tight that even the smallest inconvenience sets off a series of get-even and retaliatory reactions that not only affects us but the people we come in contact with.

I'll speak for myself when I confess that I'm a bit too serious for my own good, and for those that I come in contact with.

Here are several things that I'm attempting to do to lighten up a little.

- ➡ Ask   "So what's the big deal?"
- ➡ Ask   "Is there a funny side to this?"
- ➡ Ask   "Are there people involved who shouldn't be?"
- ➡ Ask   "How would Mother Teresa act?"

Every time we interact with another human being we experience a magic moment. For the moment to be magic, it must be shared by both people. A good laugh and a big smile are all it takes to create a magic moment.

I know it always feels better after a smile, what I'm still working on is how to give more of them.

Humor is an affirmation of dignity, a declaration of man's superiority to all that befalls him.

Romain Gary

Everything is funny as long as it is happening to somebody else.

Will Rogers

Our remedies oft in ourselves do lie.

Shakespeare

#46

Why You're Too Busy To See
The Customers You're Unwilling To Give Up

Most sales reps have too many accounts. If that's true then it means that some of those customers won't get the attention they deserve. How many sales calls did you make last year? It's easy to calculate. Start with how many days a year you are face-to-face with customers and multiply your average number of daily sales calls.

The resulting number will likely reflect the actual number of sales calls that you are making in one year, but the resulting number may not be what you were hoping to see.

Follow these steps to calculate your sales calls.

Start with 365 days.

Subtract the following:
104 weekend days,
11-13 paid holidays,
10-20 vacation days,
3-5 sick days,
25-75 administrative and office days,
10-30 training days,
and probably several goof-off days.

Jim Meisenheimer

**Multiply what's left by your average number
of sales calls per day.**

You probably have a lower and more realistic number of
annual sales calls.

What percent of your total selling time do you want to
spend calling on existing customers? What percent of your
time do want to plan for prospecting? If you're making 950
sales calls a year and you want to spend 20 percent of your
time prospecting, it means 190 of your sales calls will be
prospecting calls and the balance will be for existing
customers.

Having fun? If you're like most sales reps, you probably
have large, medium, and small accounts. How do you want
to allocate your time (sales calls) by account size? Here's a
clue. Follow the 80/20 rule. It was coined by the Italian
economist Pareto, and when applied to sales means that
20% of your accounts will give you 80% of your volume.
The same rationale could be applied to prospects. So, if you
want to invest more time with larger customers and
prospects, you should begin by rearranging your call
schedule.

A very key variable to selling success is investing the right
amount of time in the right accounts. If you have a lot of
small accounts and you're spending too much time calling
on them at the expense of priority accounts, you better
figure a way to change your call pattern.

Give up the small accounts. Stop calling on them. The
small sales returns you get don't justify the time you're

investing. Remember, you have too many big customers and big prospects to cover. Leave the small accounts for direct mail and telemarketing coverage. You should be too busy to see the small accounts you're unwilling to give up.

Application...

Calculate the number of sales calls you make a year.

> **Poor delegation is a major cause for lost time.**
> **Margaret McElroy**

> **Spilled water never returns to the cup.**
> **Japanese Proverb**

#47

How To Polish Up Your Follow-up

Why is the follow-up in sales generally thought of as something that comes at the end of a successful selling effort? Maybe it has something to do with our innate desire to follow rather than to lead. One way to be different from the masses in sales is to begin with your follow-up not merely end with it. Here are some examples.

The appointment - Whenever you get an appointment be sure to confirm it in writing. A short note card, sent with some company (not product) literature, not only confirms the meeting it shows your sense of appreciation early. It's the human touch.

The first call - This may be one of the best and only times you need to write a formal letter. For most other occasions a handwritten note will have a far greater impact. Aside from recapping several key points from the first meeting, it offers an excellent way to personally thank your prospect for his time and initial interest.

The needs assessment - Once you've adequately identified your prospective client's needs, a written or telephone follow-up will serve to clarify your understanding of their situation, demonstrate your involvement, show your interest, and create understanding while building rapport early in the sales process.

The demonstration - When you get to the demonstration phase, remember to show your gratitude and your willingness to personally respond to any unanswered questions.

The proposal - Most proposals are prepared and submitted as glorified price lists. Imagine a buyer receiving three proposals and the only thing different about them were their prices. Proposals are an opportunity to showcase your creativity and capabilities. Be sure to personalize it with their name, use color, and devote at least one full page to stating your benefits.

The order - Make sure you personally thank each customer for the business. If it's a large order, insure that someone from senior management also sends a note of appreciation.

Customer satisfaction - Avoid asking new customers how they like the new product or service. If you're really interested in the process of improvement, ask them how you and your company can make it better. It's a terrific question because it points out your soft spots.

Years ago TLC (tender loving care) was a big item in the halls of many businesses. Today, it seldom comes out of the closet to see the time of day. As we approach the 21st Century, try adding ALTC (a little touch of class) to your selling style. These personal touches will increase your visibility and rapport with most of your contacts.

In golf and in life, it's the follow through that makes the difference.

Anonymous

Compliments cost nothing, yet many pay dear for them.

German Proverb

Boldness in business is the first, second, and third thing.

Thomas Fuller

There are two fools in every market: one asks too little, one asks too much.

Russian Proverb

The Lighter Side

*"But what makes you think I'd
be any good in Sales."*

The Lighter Side

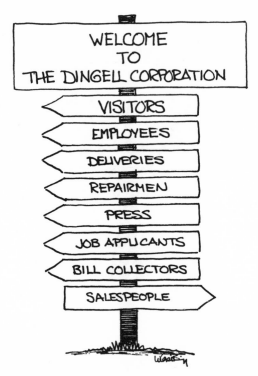

WELCOME
TO
THE DINGELL CORPORATION

VISITORS

EMPLOYEES

DELIVERIES

REPAIRMEN

PRESS

JOB APPLICANTS

BILL COLLECTORS

SALESPEOPLE

The Lighter Side

The Lighter Side

Power Selling Resource Guide

Personal Selling Power Magazine
800-752-7355

Selling Magazine
800-360-5344

Success Magazine
800-234-7324

Sales & Marketing Management Magazine
800-821-6897

Telephone Selling Report
402-895-9399

Nightingale-Conant Audio Tapes
800-525-9000

Master Salesmanship
800-345-8101

About Jim Meisenheimer

As a consultant • trainer • speaker, I've been extremely fortunate during the first five years of my business. What began as a dream, was later transformed into a goal, and is now an international business committed to helping sales professionals by changing their selling behaviors. The bedrock principle to all my programs is that to be really successful in sales you must often act counter-instinctively, and fully develop your unique selling style. There are three operating priorities for me when I'm working with a customer. More than priorities they have become imperatives. They are preparation, practice and professionalism.

As a...

Consultant - I work with organizations to help them achieve maximum productivity in critical areas. A comprehensive assessment is essential to success.

Trainer - I deliver customer specific sales and customer service training programs. These include one-half day, one day, and two day seminars.

Speaker - I present keynote (sixty to ninety minute) presentations that provide education, inspiration and motivation to corporate clients.

For more information call **(708) 680-7880.**

More Selling Success Products From Jim Meisenheimer

#1 - Sales Strategist Newsletter. This is a quarterly publication filled with new selling ideas, sales resources, timely tips and a full page of motivational and inspirational quotes. Annual subscription is $49.

#2 - How To Win More Sales audio cassette tape. This 57 minute tape is loaded with practical selling tips that will help you get the business today. $19.95.

#3 - The Ten Best Questions To Ask Customers audio cassette tape. This is a 47 minute tape that will show you how to sell more by saying less. You'll hear the best questions to ask and learn why. $19.95.

#4 - Maximum Results In Minimum Time audio cassette tape. This 50 minute tape delivers creative new ideas on how to improve your personal selling productivity. $19.95.

#5 - How To Watch Your Time And Grow Your Territory special selling report. In this 3,000 word report you'll discover new ways to deal with the old problems of managing your time. $4.50.

#6 - Twelve Ways To Create A Personal Selling Edge special selling report. This report features 12 solid ideas and techniques that will increase competence and build confidence. You'll learn and earn more. $4.50.

For ordering information see page 144

Order Form

Photocopy, FAX or return this page to: Jim Meisenheimer, JM Associates

824 Paddock • Libertyville • IL• 60048

FAX (708) 680-7881

Clearly write down the item numbers in the spaces provided.

_____ _____ _____ _____ _____

Order total here $ _____. Illinois residents must add 6.5% sales tax here $ _____. Shipping and handling (add $2.00 per audio tape and $.50 for each selling report). Total shipping and handling $ _____.
Total order is $_____.

Method of payment:
_____ prepayment (enclose check or money order).
_____ credit card (write complete number below).
check one _____Visa _____Mastercard

Credit card number _____

Expiration date is _____

    Send to:
    Name _____
    Company _____
    Street _____
    City _____State ____Zip _____
    Telephone (   ) _____
    FAX (   ) _____